THERE'S NO PLACE LIKE

HOPE

A Guide to Beating Cancer in Mind-sized Bites

✦

*A Book of Hope, Help, and Inspiration for
Cancer Patients and Their Families*

BY VICKIE GIRARD

Edited by Dan Zadra
Designed by Kobi Yamada and Steve Potter
Compendium Inc.

Praise for *There's No Place Like Hope*

Vickie Girard provides compelling examples of why Patient Empowerment Medicine works, and how it can save lives. If you are a cancer patient, or a loving caregiver, this is an inspirational and hopeful message you cannot afford to overlook.
—Richard J. Stephenson, Founder and Chairman
Cancer Treatment Centers of America

Anyone who has been touched by cancer cannot help but be affected by Vickie Girard's account of her own victory over the disease. She communicates the devastation caused by the diagnosis, engages the reader in each hurdle encountered, and shares the triumph…with strength, humor and compassion.
—Susan Root, Community Development Director,
American Cancer Society

Finally, a book that speaks to cancer patients and survivors in a way we can truly understand—I hope all cancer patients and survivors, their families, friends and caregivers have a copy of this book in their hands!
—Cheryl Caleca, Link To Life Newsletter

This book has been needed for such a long time. Not only is it a worthy companion for every person going through cancer, it is also very helpful for those of us who minister and care for them.
—Amber Laueener, Chaplain

Thank God for this inspired book. It's exactly what the doctor ordered for all patients, caregivers and loved ones fighting the good fight of faith against cancer.
—Rev. Percy W. McCray Jr., Pastor
Valor Faith Ministries

A true success story in the fight against cancer, and it all started with just a glimmer of hope that built on itself. Without hope, cancer cannot be fought. For it's hope that brings the patient into the arena to fight against it.

—Dr. Alfonso Mellijor, MD, Surgical Oncologist

There could be no more powerful proof of the power of hope than Vickie Girard's triumph over cancer. Through this book, she now offers the power of hope to others for their own battles with this horrible, but conquerable disease.

—Stephen B. Bonner, President and CEO
Cancer Treatment Centers of America

A very straightforward guide for the cancer patient, their family and friends—a book that you can open at random, put a finger on a paragraph and gain encouragement and insight every day.

—Joel Granick, MD, Medical Oncologist

Here is a wealth of insight, compassion and, yes, hope, for those who have been touched by cancer. Vickie Girard's "bite size" observations are easy to read and grasp, but filled with enough truth to ponder for days, written by a woman who has been there—and survived.

—Timothy C. Birdsall, ND, National Director
Naturopathic Medicine and Research, CTCA

For years I have searched for a book that tells people with cancer that it is okay to cry or to feel upset about having cancer, and that doing so does not mean that you are giving up hope!

—Elizabeth T. Crane, M.Ed., LCPC
Director, Mind/Body Medicine, CTCA

DEDICATION

This book is dedicated to every cancer patient it has ever been
my privilege to speak to or to meet. By sharing your stories
and experiences with me over the years, you have given me
much more than I could ever hope to give you in return. You
have opened the windows of your hearts and souls to me.
We have laughed, cried, yelled in anger and frustration at the
viciousness of this disease—together. We have celebrated
successes and mourned those who have gone before us—
together. We have become sisters and brothers bonded by fate
and experience. We have talked about everything under the
sun and in the heavens. You made me realize just how similar
we all are, regardless of the type of cancer we have. We all
have the same fears, worries, and concerns. We have all felt,
at one time or another, isolated from the "healthy" world and
wondered if anyone really understands. We got lucky, we
spoke to each other, and in doing so, validated our own
feelings—and found that it helped more than we could have
ever imagined.

It is because of this that I wrote *There's No Place Like Hope*.
Thank you all for having so enriched my life with your spirit
and sharing.

ISBN: 1-888387-41-6
©2001 Vickie Girard and Compendium, Inc. All rights reserved.
Written permission must be secured from the publisher to use or
reproduce any part of this book. Contact: Compendium, Inc., 6325
212th St. SW, Suite K, Lynnwood, WA 98036. There's No Place Like
Hope, the format, illustrations, layout and coloring used in this book
are trademarks and/or trade dress of Compendium, Inc.

Printed in China

TABLE OF CONTENTS

There's No Place Like Hope is written for every person who has ever had to hear a cancer diagnosis. Please know that you are not alone; others too have felt as you are feeling and come out the other side stronger. This is not a cliche, this is fact. You don't have to believe me yet—as a matter of fact, I'm sure you don't—but it is the truth. By the end of this book I hope that you can *feel* it for yourself.

A friend of mine recently shared a proverb with me: "To know the road ahead, ask those coming back." I really like those words. They pretty much sum up my purpose in writing this book, but maybe not in the way you are imagining. This is not another "story of my life" book. I don't see how the nuts and bolts of my disease—how large my tumors were, or what my counts were, or how many days I spent in bone marrow transplant—would necessarily help you in your struggle. The mechanics of your disease will differ from mine even if our cancer is the same.

Don't get me wrong, I think we need all the success stories we can hear. But I think there are already enough books out there about individual victories over cancer. I have always felt that success in beating cancer lies in the bigger issues that we all face, rather than in the details. For, if success was all in the details, how could my success with breast cancer be encouraging to an ovarian, or a colon, or a prostate or a lung patient—and yet it has been countless times.

There's No Place Like Hope is meant to be a book of sharing. It is a book about a journey that I have tried to record, not day by day, but more feeling by feeling, awakening by awakening. It is not my journey alone, but the combined journeys of many. I write a column called "Vickie's Spin" and I guess that's what this is—my spin on dealing successfully with cancer. For deal with it I have.

This is a book of my thoughts—thoughts that I once believed were mine alone, but I now know that only the wording is my own. For over the last ten years I've spoken to literally thousands of cancer patients and survivors. And I've learned that we are all more alike than we could ever imagine. I learned, too, that it helps to know that others have felt as we feel and have not just survived, but have found ways to be enriched by the experience. To do that, we must share.

If you are reading this, as of this minute, you are no longer alone in your feelings. In the darkness of the night or in the sometimes too harsh brightness of day, know that I and others, too, have been there. When you wonder if anyone has ever felt what you are feeling, know that we have. When your loving family and well-meaning friends are still not enough, and you pray for someone to understand, know that we do. I believe with all my heart that God places people in our path when we need them the most. They sometimes come to us in person, sometimes by phone or in a letter, and sometimes in a book. Through this book, He just placed me in yours.

I come with vital information to share with cancer patients at any stage of your battle, regardless of the type of cancer. There are ways of looking at the battle that can make an incredible difference, not only in the final outcome, but in surviving each day of the struggle. I believe that cancer is fought on three battlefields—your mind, your heart, and your body. I also believe that it is fought in that order. For it is the mind that screams and the heart that cries, when it is still hard to believe that our body has cancer.

I have subtitled this book, "Beating Cancer in Mind-sized Bites," for I believe that is how cancer is really beaten. For you to defeat this disease, you must be able to reduce diagnosis, treatment, and day-to-day living to a "doable" size. But even before that can be done, there must first be one essential thing—and that is HOPE.

This is first, last, and always a book of hope. It is a book of finding that sometimes tiny spark and learning how to fan it into a flame. It is a *learned* process. I know because from the very depths of despair I learned to hope again and then to find joy in life again—even during a tremendous cancer battle.

I call hope my "pilot light" because I now know that, without it, we truly cease to exist. Personally, I believe that our pilot light is lit by God at the moment of our birth and it is the only thing that accompanies our souls back home. But hope, like any pilot light, must be protected and fed. It is not something you either have or don't have. It is something that can be adjusted and rekindled—it can even be relit. This, too, is something I had to learn along the way: *Let no one ever steal your hope, or extinguish your pilot light!*

Maybe now is a good time for us to take a little journey together. Time to tell you a little of who I am and of how I earned my stripes in this war. As I said, this is not "My Life's Story," but I think you must know something of my battle in order to have confidence in my conclusions. By sharing a few details of my own struggles with this disease, I hope to give you additional confidence for yours. This is the shorthand version, the "Cliff's Notes," if you will. So take my hand and let's journey down the road that ultimately led me to this book and into your life.

How I Earned My Stripes

In the spring of 1989 I found a lump in my breast, seven months after a clear mammogram. I would have a partial mastectomy with 21 lymph nodes removed. I had no lymph node involvement and no follow up treatment was recommended. I was 36 years old.

About a year and a half later I began experiencing shoulder pain. Over the next seven months I would see five doctors, each time expressing my fears that the pain could be a symptom of breast-to-bone cancer, and each time being assured that it wasn't. I even passed my critical two-year checkup with flying colors; they said my shoulder pain was probably a touch of arthritis. When the pain persisted, I finally saw an orthopedic surgeon who, at last, sent me for my first bone scans.

I tell you now with the deepest conviction, if you ever sense that something is wrong, make your doctors rule out your fears with tests and not opinions. Failure to do so almost cost me my life. The bone scans would show five spots of cancer; my sternum, first rib, head, neck, and shoulder were all affected. I had lost seven months in which I could have been fighting it—seven months in which it had been allowed to grow. I was devastated.

I rushed back to the cancer facility where I had had my original surgery and they confirmed the diagnosis. When I asked how bad it was, they told me "very." It was the tone more than the word, and it was the atmosphere in the room that led me to ask, "Are you saying this is going to kill me?" They answered, "Yes." Period. Point blank. Not, "I am so sorry." Not, "That remains to be seen." Not, "It could kill you, if we don't begin treatment." Just, "Yes."

I then asked the million dollar question: "How much time do I have?" They said they wanted to remove my ovaries and start hormonal treatment. If this slowed the progression of the disease I could possibly get 18 months, but probably closer to a year. If it failed to slow the progression, then six months was more realistic. Later in this book you will read how destructive I believe "time limits" are. I believe there is a real danger in their becoming a self-fulfilling prophecy. That office visit in January of 1992 almost killed me, long before the cancer could, for it almost destroyed my will to fight. I had walked into that office thinking of what I would have to do to live, and ten minutes later all I could think about was dying. That ten minutes did more damage than the cancer, for it *almost* did what the cancer had not done—it *almost* stole my hope.

One of the most important things that I learned on this journey is that no one but God knows how many days any of us are meant to walk this earth. Not a doctor, not a hospital, not even we ourselves. As Gracie Allen once said, "Never place a period in your life where God only meant to place a comma." I couldn't agree more. But in 1992 that beautiful insight was still far in the future for me, a future that didn't look at all promising.

I had the surgery, my ovaries were removed, and I was sent home and told to return in three months. I asked about chemotherapy and was told that it was not recommended at this time. When I asked about vitamins, I was told to take a One-A-Day if I wanted to. Surely, this couldn't be the only thing available to me. There had to be *something* more that I could do.

Over the next three months my husband, Rick, and I would call, visit, send slides and scans to some of the most prestigious cancer centers in this country. I learned to be very pushy and persuasive. I got through to some of the biggest names in cancer research, but always with the same discouraging results, predictions, and time limits. They wouldn't recommend anything that my own hospital wasn't already doing. In desperation I tried to participate in experimental cancer studies and trials and became more depressed when even they didn't want me. I now understand that future grant money is based on successful studies—and I didn't look like a potential success to anyone.

The point that was coming through loud and clear was that everyone thought it was senseless to keep trying. The outcome had already been written in those initial dire statistics. Once I was considered terminal it became crystal clear that everyone was working on the premise that I would die. Every bit of advice, recommendation, and suggestion was based on the assumption of death. Treatment was pointless because…. Nutrition was pointless because…. Vitamins were pointless because…. The groundwork was being laid for me to do nothing but die. If we follow clear-cut directions to a predetermined destination, chances are we will reach it. And the directions for me now led to death. But through it all I just kept thinking, "What if we could just find someone who would believe in the possibility, if not the probability, that I could live?"

In Search Of Hope

My husband, Rick, had always believed in the untapped power of our own immune systems. For years he had studied vitamin and nutritional advances as a hobby, and

I had only half listened. Now his hobby became a passion. His new mission was to empower my God-given immune system to fight back. He researched everything he could get his hands on. How could we combine standard oncology procedures with aggressive nutritional practices? Rick was learning at breakneck speed, but we knew nothing of chemotherapy. We felt as if we were trying to conduct the Boston Philharmonic without knowing how to read music. Time was running out.

Then more bad news: Just weeks into my own battle, Rick's mother was diagnosed with the same disease. We were devastated. The pressure to find effective treatment increased, for Margaret was quickly losing ground. Within weeks she was admitted to the hospital for pain control. Our lives had become a living nightmare. It was at this incredibly dark point that I believe God sent us a miracle—not in the form of the biblical burning bush, but in the form of a modern 60-second television commercial.

Rick had come home from the hospital one afternoon to shower and change. I fixed him a sandwich and gave it to him on a paper plate. He sat down in front of the television. Suddenly he called for me to come quick. There was a commercial about a woman who had had cancer, had been given up, but had survived by going to this hospital. It was called the Cancer Treatment

Centers of America. They said they believed in treating the whole person, not just the tumor. (How novel.) Yes, they used chemotherapy, radiation, and surgery, but they also used nutrition as part of the treatment. They believed in empowering our own immune systems to fight the disease. It sounded like everything we had been searching for.

Rick wrote the number on the edge of his paper plate (I've always wondered what would have happened had I used a real plate) and handed it to me to make the call while he returned to the hospital to be with Margaret. At this point, I hadn't yet summoned the courage to tell him I had already decided there would be no more calls. But even though I was sure this, too, would turn out to be pointless, I took a chance and called. I am alive today because I did.

That call was like none of the others I had made. A very kind and knowledgeable woman spoke to me for over an hour and patiently answered all my questions. Cancer Treatment Centers of America already had in place the philosophy that we had been desperately searching for. All areas of wellness would be brought into play to fight in harmony against the disease. It sounded as if we had finally found the conductor for our music. Not only were they using all the available instruments, but they were designing some of their own.

It would turn out to be too late for Rick's mom. We lost her a few days later. But that phone call gave us something to hang on to during the difficult days that followed. Cancer Treatment Centers of America became a touchstone for us all. Yes I would go, but secretly I was thinking, "What can this hospital do that all the others could not?" Nevertheless, just days after burying Rick's mom we were there.

We arrived at CTCA as many do, emotionally and physically exhausted, with our spirits, if not yet broken, then very badly bruised. We came hoping for miracles, but expecting the same old thing—and we couldn't have been more wrong. After that first morning I still wasn't sure if this place could save me, but I knew they were different. The first doctor we saw, Dr. Alfonso Mellijor, was God-sent. He said that they had looked at my scans, reviewed my reports…and then he said the magic words, he thought that they could help me. I had held on for so long. I had refused to cry with each death sentence and now someone was giving us hope and I simply broke down. So much had been riding on the first words he spoke. Usually those words had been, "I'm sorry."

Over the next hour and a half Dr. Mellijor didn't sugar coat the negative, but he did an amazing thing—he emphasized the positive. I can't tell you what a differ ence that made. He suggested a year of aggressive chemotherapy with nutritional support. A *year*. No one else had thought I would still be alive in a year! Even though the hormonal treatment had failed and I had additional spots, he told me he did not believe I was hopeless; in fact, he was trying to convince me I *wasn't* hopeless. This was a switch. He was so calm about it all; they actually had a plan.

Now, did all of this make me jump for joy and sign on the dotted line? No, I was cautiously impressed with everything I had seen and heard. I did believe that they were different and I wished that we had found them sooner. Yes, but could *all* those other hospitals have been wrong? For months the hope had been stamped out of me everywhere I turned. I had even been warned to "watch out" for hospitals that would be willing to make promises that they couldn't keep and take my last dollar as I died. Was I skeptical? You bet I was, but I was listening.

Dr. Mellijor told me right up front that he couldn't predict the outcome, but he said that there was one thing he *could* promise. Every day that I chose to fight, he promised that he would fight with me and for me with everything at his disposal and anything that he could find. Later, as he got ready to leave the room, he stopped and said that he had made me a promise—now he wanted one from me. He said, "Vickie, if you choose not to fight here, that's fine. But promise me that you won't give up because I believe you have a chance, I believe that there is hope."

Hope—what a wonderful, beautiful word it is. I hadn't understood until that moment that all my deepest emotions had evolved around that little word. The roller coaster ride that had become my life had all been driven by the loss of, and the renewed search for— hope. Yes, I would've loved a guarantee that I would get well, but I knew that was impossible. What I had been searching for was hope. So many doctors had been so busy telling me what I couldn't do. They had been so concerned about protecting me from "false" hope, that they had done the worst imaginable thing—they had left me with no hope at all. Without hope I could find no foothold, nothing to stop my spiraling, downward fall.

I thank God nightly that CTCA recognized that nothing good, nothing healthy can live in this state. They understood that not just my body was sick, but that my mind was tired, confused, and frightened. Slowly, with kindness, compassion, and medical expertise second to none they helped me to again become a *living,* breathing person—a person with a problem and a potential solution—and not just a dying patient with no hope.

I would eventually undergo an aggressive program of eleven months of chemotherapy, hormonal, nutritional, and naturopathy treatments, at all times supported by a PNI department (mind/body medicine) and spiritual support second to none. I found that there is never just one way of looking at a problem, but many. This new way of thinking helped me find alternate ways of seeing treatment, as well as life during treatment. And it was working! In three months all my tumors were contained; in six months all showed healing; in nine months the smallest ones were gone and the largest ones were smaller. They then began talking about a bone marrow transplant, something no one else had ever thought I would qualify for. In May of 1993 I had that transplant (thank you Drs. Bolwell and Lichten) and I have been totally cancer-free ever since.

It was a long process, but the day my hope was first fed is the day I began to get well. I now know that the heart and the mind must first seek and believe in health in order for the body to find it. For many battles are won or lost because of this little word. Remembering the dire statistics that were quoted to me, I've often wondered what would become of those statistics if every cancer patient was encouraged and supported in their fight as I eventually was?

I often think of cancer patients as injured birds, for I know that's how I once felt—fragile, frightened, and searching. Some of us have broken wings and some have wings that are just muddied, but it matters not which, for you can fly with neither. I believe that it is hope that can quiet our spirits long enough for the mud of desperation to be cleansed away so that, God-willing, our wings can be mended and we can fly again.

There's No Place Like Hope is meant to do just that—to quiet your mind and heart with a real and practical message of hope. To share with you that even the worst of odds can be beaten and overcome. I write to tell you that, yes, I have been down the road and I've come back to tell you where the monsters most often lurk and what it is that *they* are afraid of. I'm here to remind you that, if you look closely, there are bread crumbs along the path so that you will know that others, too, have traveled it and survived.

I will not tell you that you won't feel helpless at times, for I know far too well that feeling. What I am telling you is that you can climb back out of that dark pit of despair—that hope exists for all of us. Hope led me to dream of wellness, and the dream of wellness sustained me throughout the realities of treatment.

So keep your pilot light burning brightly. Guard it, nurture it, protect and fan it with success stories. And know that I'm with you all the way.

Vickie Girard

I know God won't

give me anything

I can't handle,

I just wish He didn't

trust me so much.

—*Mother Teresa*

CONFRONTING THE BULLY

*I describe "cancer" as the one word in the entire
English language that the mind sees in all capital letters.
May this book help all who read it to change the case,
reduce the size and the power of the word itself, so that
we may all better fight and better survive this disease.*

❦

Cancer! In the space of time it takes to utter the word,
it tries to steal your way of life and your peace of mind.
We must begin our fight against cancer here first, in our
minds.

❦

Cancer must be fought mind, body, and soul. After all, it
is first the mind that screams, and the heart and soul
that cry out, long before the body hurts.

❦

Your mind and your heart will be either your greatest
allies or your most formidable foes. They will never,
ever be ignored.

❦

Grasp a new perception of this disease by looking at
what it is not; what it has not. Cancer does not have a
brain, or a heart, or a spirit. It doesn't have the ability to

plan or be cunning. It doesn't have a heart that causes it to fight, or a spirit that gives it the reason to. It is you who has the brain, the ability to strategize. It is you who has the ability to plan its demise. And it is you who has the heart and the soul to bring to this fight.

≝

I have often thought of cancer as the schoolyard bully. He's a bully with such a bad reputation that he no longer has to fight; just the mere thought of him can send people running. But all it takes is for a couple of people to stand up to the bully to diminish his reputation. That's what a cancer success story does—it stares down the cancer bully. It shows that he can be beaten—and, believe me, he can!

≝

Remember always, cancer is only a small part of who and what you are—never the sum total.

≝

We have cancer—cancer does not have us.

≝

We are living with—not dying of—cancer.

≝

CONFRONTING THE BULLY

We must stop speaking of cancer in whispers, as if it is something shameful. For when it is brought out into the brilliant light of day it seems to shrink, to pull back, to diminish.

🌿

Above all, know this: Cancer is a beatable, treatable, survivable disease.

DIAGNOSIS

Every battle begins with the first step. With diagnosis, you've already taken it.

🌿

Immediately throw out any old cancer horror stories. Times, treatments, and diagnoses are all changing and improving as we speak!

🌿

People have told me that they fear diagnosis so much, that they don't want to know if something is wrong. Try to look at diagnosis as an alarm that has gone off in your home. An intruder, a thief has entered. Is the house lost? Of course not! It is sad that you have been broken into, but thank God the alarm sounded so you can get help, stop the invader, and save your treasures. With diagnosis you just got lucky. A known enemy is always better than an unknown one. Now you can begin to fight back, regain control.

🌿

That *sick* feeling in the pit of your stomach will go away. Believe it or not, the first days after diagnosis are the worst. I know that is hard to believe. When you're first diagnosed you're thinking, "Oh, my God, and this is just the beginning—how am I ever going to get through this?" The shock, the panic, and the paralysis will wear off. For now, trust me on this, diagnosis is about as bad as it gets.

❧

Remember, you are no sicker the day of diagnosis than you were the day before.

❧

Diagnosis is like going to sleep in your own bed and waking up in a foreign country where you don't know the language or the customs and you have no maps telling you how to get home.

❧

Gather information! With diagnosis came treatment options, and I felt as if huge decisions were being left in my totally incapable hands. I was right; I didn't, at that time, have enough knowledge to make any informed decision. Except in extreme cases, take the time after diagnosis and before treatment to gather all the information you can. Get on the internet, call the Cancer Treatment Resource Center, and get a second opinion.

❧

DIAGNOSIS

I'll say it again—get a second opinion. No matter how much you trust, love, or respect your physician, he or she can only bring to you what they have seen, done, heard, or read about. An individual decision is based on only two eyes, two ears, two hands, and one brain. At the very *least*, bring in four eyes, four ears, four hands, and two brains.

※

People are often afraid of insulting their physician by asking for their medical records so that they can get a second opinion, but a good, confident doctor will never be insulted by your needing more information. If he or she will not welcome any new insight that may improve your chances for recovery, then it is best to learn this now. A question to ask yourself: "If my physician doesn't want me asking anyone else's opinion, does that mean that my options run out if his ideas do?"

※

I believe that second opinions should come from different areas of the country if at all possible. Get an idea of what is being done in other regions. A second opinion doesn't mean that you won't return to your original physician. If you do, I guarantee that you will do so with even more confidence.

※

DIAGNOSIS

The cost of a second consultation is sometimes the best money you will ever spend.

✺

Don't buy into time limits, for they tend to become a self-fulfilling prophecy.

✺

Time limits—what is their point? Would we not die if they didn't tell us when to do so? If that is the case, maybe we have just cured cancer!

✺

I wish all doctors would be as careful of their words as they are of their medication. The side effects of medication will eventually wear off, but it took many months before I could begin to shed the effect of the word "terminal."

✺

There are all kinds of shock. When patients go into shock from trauma, they are kept warm, spoken to calmly, monitored for response. They are wrapped in a cocoon of support until the immediate crisis passes. Wouldn't it be nice if there were a procedure to treat the *shock* of a cancer diagnosis? Even the most basic, commonsense rules would help: Don't tell a person that they have cancer when they are alone or on the phone. Immediately provide them with the telephone number of a good support group, contact person, or therapist. Have a knowledgeable professional right there to answer their questions and get their feet back on the ground (thank you, Doctor M and Doctor Sanchez). Have a suggested course of action. And, yes, a warm hug would go a long way, too.

⚘

A woman called me one day and said her doctors had given her a death sentence. They had told her that she wouldn't live two years with what she had. HOW DARE THEY! Who knows where medicine will be a year from now or a month from now? What if she makes a choice not to continue to fight because of their diagnoses? What if a cure or treatment is found in the next year or two and she is no longer here?

⚘

One last thing on time limits, my pet peeve: A doctor once told me that it is we, the patients, who often ask, "How much time do I have?" He asked, "What should I do—lie to you?" He is right. We often do ask that question in a moment of panic, in the wave of first knowledge. Of course doctors should not lie to us. They are our physicians and we must trust them. They should tell us the truth and only the truth. If our disease is life threatening, tell us so that we can aggressively fight. But tell us the whole truth. The whole truth is that the end remains to be written; for neither we, nor they, are God.

🌿

The thought of dying from cancer scares everyone, that is a given—but that's not the sad part. What is sad is that the fear sometimes causes people to give up their lives without a fight. I've met patients who are already gone in their minds—they are just waiting for their body to catch up. I want to shake them, for they are throwing away exactly what they are so afraid of losing.

🌿

Even if you *think* you only have six months left don't stop fighting unless you yourself choose to, and then think twice. For me, not fighting during the four months that I was convinced I had a death sentence hanging over my head was much harder than any portion of the battle in which I actively fought.

🌿

When I was first diagnosed, I felt as if cancer was destroying me by the second. I began to think that my body had betrayed me. In my mind, my body had become the enemy. It is easy to think this way, but dangerous. I eventually chose to look at my body as a sponge, and cancer as water in the sponge. Now push all the water (cancer) down from your head, up your arms into your trunk, up one leg and all down into the other. Now even at my worst, cancer would only have come from, say, my foot to my knee. Now look back at all that is healthy and realize that you have a God-given immune system built in to every healthy cell to help you rid yourself of the cancer. Realize that the majority of your body is healthy!

❦

Regardless of the diagnosis, each and every day that we breathe we are living with—not dying of—cancer. (Otherwise, we have been dying of *life* since the day we were born.)

❦

Choose to live each day fully, not merely to draw one day closer to death, for it is within the day's journey that life's treasures lie.

❦

Even when it is not probable, it is still possible to win against this disease. I am living proof of this.

❦

The moment you survive the diagnosis you become a survivor. The moment your cancer has been detected, your success story begins.

❦

HOPE

Hope is the foundation on which we build our wellness. It is our most vital emotion.

✺

My continued existence sprang from hope put into action.

✺

I call hope my pilot light, for I now know that without it I truly cease to exist. Let no one ever steal your hope, or put out your pilot light.

✺

Like all pilot lights, hope must be fueled and protected in order to survive. Feed it positive thoughts and success stories. Protect it with sound information and knowledge.

✺

Try to see hope in all capital letters. HOPE. There, doesn't that look better?

✺

Hope is the voice that God uses to speak to our hearts instead of our heads.

✺

HOPE

Hope is God's parachute in life. Hope is when God smiles.

✤

Hope must be there in the beginning for us to start. It is a well from which we must continuously drink to refresh and sustain ourselves.

✤

If you don't feel hopeless, you won't feel helpless.

✤

It's even written in the book of all books, the Bible: "With hope, all things are possible."

✤

God gives us hope when He gives us life. When we are newborns we hope to be picked up, changed, and fed. What we hope for will change a thousand times throughout our lives, but with the very last breath we draw we still will be hoping.

✤

God lit a candle of hope for each of us. It's not waiting in a window somewhere, or around a bend. He lit it right inside us so that we need not ever live one moment without it.

✤

HOPE

Hope and positivity are two different things. You can have hope and not be positive every single day, but you can't have a single moment of positivity without hope.

❧

I do not believe that a person can be healed "in spite of themselves." Instead, I believe that healing must come by restoring the essence of self. It is only through hoping for health that we have any chance of restoring it.

❧

There is no such thing as "false hope." Hope is not a product, but a process. Hope is not contingent on any outcome.

❧

Hope makes you reach when you know your arm is too short. Hope gives you that extra, added stretch to reach it after all.

❧

Hope is a prayer without the formality.

❧

Hope costs nothing to give and is priceless to have.

❧

HOPE

Hope is exercise for the spirit; it swings open the door to possibilities.

🌾

With hope, the imagination soars.

🌾

Hope is like a gift, both to give and receive.

🌾

My little niece, Chelsea, once gave us a lesson on hope. She was *hoping* for something that her mom and all of us pretty much thought was impossible. Trying to protect her from being disappointed, Chelsea's mom tried to re-direct her, only to have my niece say that no one has the right to tell you that you can't hope or what you should hope for—and she was going to keep right on hoping. How right she was! No one has the right to steal your hope or re-direct it. By the way, Chelsea's high hopes proved us all wrong, and she eventually got exactly what she was hoping for.

🌾

I've learned that it is the undying hope of something that makes the dream possible. And it is the dream of that something that eventually leads to its reality.

🌾

TREATMENT

Treatment is *not* worse than the disease!

❧

We didn't get cancer overnight nor will we always be able to get rid of it overnight. But with diagnosis and treatment we are on the way to being healthier than we have been in months and probably years. We are also safer, we can no longer be ambushed. As I said earlier, a known enemy is always better that an unknown one.

❧

I learned very early to look at what surgery, chemo, or radiation was going to do *for* me instead of to me. That made all the difference.

❧

Cancer treatment is like going to war. You want to win, so you want to be well armed. There are many weapons at your disposal: surgery, chemo, radiation, nutrition, naturopathy, hormonal therapy, immunology, mind/body medicine and, of course, spiritual support. Be prepared to understand and use any and all weapons in an appropriate way. You want to take the combined forces of the Army, Navy, Air Force, and Marines into battle with you. In other words, "Don't put all your eggs in *any* one basket."

❧

Myth: All cancer treatment is the same. **Truth:** The field of cancer treatment is wide and varied. You should choose the battlefield on which you wage your war very carefully. The terrain can make all the difference.

※

Make sure that the treatment facility you choose opens doors for you—not closes them.

※

We often shop for our homes, cars, and even our clothing more carefully than we do our doctors and hospitals. I would never walk up to the first rack of dresses, pick the first one off the rack, and say that I might as well take it because they are all the same. No, I shop. I try different dresses on for size, and see how I feel in them. Well, the choice of a doctor is far more important. Try at least two on for fit and comfort. Remember to check their credentials and experience in your particular field of need. The right fit makes all the difference.

※

Controversial cures or home remedies: I've been at this for a long time and have talked to thousands of cancer patients. I hate to say it, but I have found no "magic bullet." Be very careful of any one product or procedure that promises to cure you. If someone actually had a single "cure-all," the lines outside their door would far surpass the breadlines of the 1930's.

🌾

Example: One woman told me her mother had cured her own breast cancer. When I asked where she had her mammogram and biopsy done, it turned out she never had either. All she knew was that her mother once had a lump and now it was gone; she just "felt sure" it was cancer. Now the daughter had been formally diagnosed with breast cancer and wanted to use her mother's home remedy. Very dangerous.

When looking at "alternative treatments" ask yourself one question: "Am I running to a particular alternative because I believe it works, or am I running away from conventional treatment because I'm so frightened of it?" Be honest with your answer—your life may depend on it.

🌾

Ignorance is not bliss; it can kill you.

🌾

Fear doesn't defeat cancer; empowered treatment defeats cancer.

🌾

TREATMENT

I've been asked what I did differently than other women who may have faced the same grim statistics that I faced. Answer: I've incorporated an informed, patient-empowered, "whole body" approach to the treatment of cancer. I took the drugs necessary to destroy the tumor, and at the same time Cancer Treatment Centers of America worked with me to change the host. I'm the host, but this host has taken down the "Cancer Welcome" sign. Will I stay cancer-free forever? Only God knows the answer, but the last seven years sure have been great.

❦

You're in charge. Remember that your treatment has a beginning and it also has an ending. I almost didn't start because I wasn't sure I could do the full year of required treatment. How silly. After all, I wasn't leasing a car (*that*, you are locked into)—I was only fighting for my life. Since I was only fighting for my life, I could stop treatment at any time. I could make the choice every day as to whether I would continue to fight. Each day I said, "Today I choose to fight, and tomorrow I'll decide." But "tomorrow" always turned into "today"—and today never seemed like a good time to stop. Leave the ending open if you must, but step into the beginning or the ending is already written!

❦

TREATMENT

Patience please. It took nine months the first time around to grow the baby that you became. You are once again renewing yourself, so be patient. No treatment lasts forever.

※

Take treatment one day at a time. Sounds easier than it is. I once tried to swallow the prescribed "year" of treatment all at one time—and nearly choked. Some things can be accomplished by the day or even by the hour that would seem impossible to do in any longer terms. Question: How do you eat an elephant? Answer: A bite at a time.

※

Cut your worries down to size. Many people take on three kinds of worry at one time. They worry about all that has happened, all that is happening, and all that might happen in their treatment. My advice is to take your worries one at a time and try not to obsess about the magnitude of your entire treatment. Yesterday is gone and tomorrow is yet to be. Today is more than enough for most of us to handle.

※

Control what you can. During treatment you will discover that there are many things you can't change—

so focus on the things you can change. Every morning ask yourself, "What can I do today to make myself happier, more fulfilled?" Sometimes it's as simple as choosing to call a friend or go to a movie.

My take on chemo: I was once asked on a survivor's panel what one can expect from chemotherapy. I knew what they wanted to hear, but after thinking about it I chose to answer it this way: What can one expect from chemo? In many, many, many cases one can expect the chemo to kill the cancer—one can expect to get well!

When we were little kids we wanted to know "why?" That's a good practice for cancer patients, too. I have found that understanding how and why a particular treatment works makes it easier to do it and appreciate it.

For example, we all want to put off our chemo treatments at one time or another. I know that doctors often forget to explain to their patients why this is not a good idea. The reason chemo is given in 21-day intervals is because healthy cells rebound in about that amount of time while the tumor cells are still reeling. Getting another treatment before the tumor cells have time to recuperate is like kicking them while they're down—which always seemed like a great idea to me. Hope this makes chemo more "user friendly" and makes you less likely to give the cancer cells time to rest by skipping a treatment.

※

If a bone marrow transplant is recommended:
First and foremost change your mind set. If your doctor suggests BMT, it does not necessarily mean you are at the end of the line. Actually it may be suggested to keep you from *reaching* the end of the line. We now realize that a bone marrow transplant is a form of treatment that may be more effective when done earlier. Suggesting BMT may be a very good thing.

※

BMT is no picnic, this is true, but the process is usually only 28 days long. You can do anything for one month.

※

Knowing what I now know, would I elect to do BMT again? Yes, absolutely yes. That should tell you a lot.

※

TREATMENT

Sometimes during treatment and all that it entails we feel very foggy. That's okay—just remember that the sun is out there shining, just waiting for you as soon as this temporary fog lifts.

※

While fighting cancer we often feel like pole-vaulters. We jump every day; it's just that life keeps raising the height of the bar.

※

Some days you fight totally for others' sake.

※

The dream of wellness sustained me throughout the reality of treatment.

※

Cancer is a serious, often life-threatening interruption and challenge. But it is also an opportunity to discover some amazing and wonderful things about yourself. I know you don't want to hear that little fact—it doesn't help much right now—but you'll be more and more convinced of it as you move through your treatment.

※

Food for thought: I'm often asked if nutrition is important. My answer, "Only if you want to live."

❦

I find it so amazing that more emphasis is not put on human diet. If the plants in our yard start to die, or our lawn gets sick, we call the nursery. They ask us to bring in a sample of the soil so they can see which nutrients the plant is getting (or not getting). If our pets get sick, the first thing the vet asks is, "What are you feeding them?" But, when we get sick, does anyone ever stop to ask, "What are you eating or not eating?"

❦

When I was re-diagnosed with cancer my prognosis was very poor, to put it mildly. I was told that this cancer would kill me—that's about as poor as it gets. I was told that chemotherapy would only ruin the quality of what little quantity I had left. I was rapidly losing weight. When I asked if I should be taking any supplements I was told, "Take One-A-Day if you want to—it can't hurt anything."

Good Lord, even I knew I was a long way away from a One-A-Day being of any help. They might as well have told me to chew two Flintstones vitamins. When I asked what I should be eating, they told me to eat everything and anything I wanted. A half-joke was made that I had a license to eat as much chocolate cake and as many french fries as I wanted. I guess this was the "up" side of a terminal diagnosis (or maybe a prescription for one). At any rate it was not the procedure I chose to follow.

❦

Before I was diagnosed, my husband's hobby was nutrition; overnight he turned it into a passion. He started me on high-dose vitamin supplements before we found anyone willing to treat me. He also taught me to respect the power of my own immune system. This concept helped give me hope in myself at a time when no one gave me much hope in anything else. Thank you, Rick, for your tireless research on my behalf. I will forever believe that the vitamins and supplements I took during treatment helped me to hold my own long enough for the chemotherapy to be effective.

❦

Dr. Patrick Quillin, a world-renowned nutritionist, and a dear friend of mine, has written many wonderful books, including my favorite, *Beating Cancer With Nutrition*. One chapter shows a tree with a fungus growing on it. Dr. Quillin writes that you can burn, cut, or poison the fungus away, but if you don't change the *fundamental environment* the tree is growing in, the fungus will likely return.

Makes sense doesn't it? Until you change the environment, everything that made the original fungus grow still remains in place, thereby creating a good possibility for reoccurrence. I couldn't agree more. I've had cancer twice. The first time I had the tumor removed and went on my merry way. Not the second time! This time, after poisoning the tumor away, I have decided to change the environment which was conducive to tumor growth—*me*.

❧

Dr. Quillin has a saying I just love: "If you have mice in your garage and you throw in a hand grenade, chances are you will kill the mice, but you'll probably lose the garage, too." He is referring to the downright questionable practice of tossing chemotherapy into the body without vitamin and nutritional support. Certain nutrients can also make the chemo a more selective toxin. *Moral:* Before we try to kill the mice, let's strengthen the garage.

❧

To me, the right kind of vitamin therapy is like putting bulletproof vests on my healthy cells.

❋

Another true story from Dr. Quillin (you must read his book!): He and his wife Noreen were in a wildlife park in San Diego. Right next to the primate enclosure they saw a bank of vending machines, filled with pop, candy, chips, ice cream, the usual. Above these machines was a sign: "Please do not feed this food to the animals, for they may get sick and die." As Dr. Quillin watched a small child partaking of one of the treats, he wondered what ingredients could be good for this 40-pound child that could potentially kill the 400-pound gorilla next door. He said the answer was simple—*none*.

❋

I'm not sure God did us a favor by letting our bodies run for so long on junk food. We begin to think that the dire effects will never catch up—but they do.

❋

A study by the National Institutes of Health in Washington, D.C., concluded that 40 percent of all cancer patients die of malnutrition. Now, doesn't that seem like a statistic we can change? Just think how great it would be if we could actually remove that 40 percent from any cancer mortality equation. Doesn't that make broccoli sound just a little better?

✻

Do I like the taste of broccoli and spinach more since I've had cancer and learned how good they are for me? No, not really, but I guess I hate them less.

✻

It may sound crazy to you, but one of the most difficult nutritional practices for me is drinking lots of water. I tried to point out to Dr. Quillin that Diet Coke is *mostly* water. He very firmly informed me that this does not count. Make sure your body is 75 percent water, not 75 percent Diet Coke.

✻

I have a sweet tooth. When I finally understood that sugar is a tumor feeder, I started visualizing what it was I was feeding (other than my sweet tooth) by consuming sugar. It made it easier to deny my tumors the chocolate cake, rather than myself.

✻

Taking vitamins and eating right was empowering for me. Each time I did so, I felt that I was fueling my immune system to fight back. I felt as if my poor immune system had been trying to fight cancer with sticks and stones because it had been so weakened by poor diet and nutrition. Mind you, I wasn't eating any worse than two-thirds of America—that is what is really frightening!

✻

When I began to feed my immune system properly it began to first hold its own, then to fight back, and then to overcome! It is amazing what a well-fed army with the latest weaponry can accomplish. With diet, exercise, and supplementation, I began training, supplying, and sustaining my immune system so that it could do what God had intended it to do—protect and serve me.

✻

No Olympic athlete would even attempt any of their events without having their body in peak condition. It doesn't matter how well you skate, swim, jump, or run— if your body isn't in shape, you'll fail because your body won't hold out long enough for your talent to prevail. Cancer may be your life's Olympics. If you must run the race, you might as well shoot for the gold!

✻

SIDE EFFECTS

You'd be amazed at how many people deny themselves the benefit of treatment simply because they fear the side effects. Let me repeat: *Treatment is not worse than the disease!* Are there side effects? Yes, but most can now be controlled. Five or ten years ago your Uncle Charlie may have been miserably ill during his cancer treatment, but that doesn't mean you will be.

❦

By law your doctor must give you the entire list of all the side effects that "could" happen with any given drug. In the studies, some patients experienced one side effect, others experienced another, etc., etc. So many side effects are listed, but this doesn't necessarily mean that you will experience all of them.

Do I sound like one of those "healthy ones" giving you the you-can-do-it lecture? I wouldn't do that to you. What I'm saying is that I've "been there, done that" and it's not as bad as you fear. There isn't any side effect you can't handle to get well again. Let's take a closer look:

Hair Loss: This was a tough one for me (see next section), but I can honestly say that the dread of losing your hair is worse than having it gone. I promise.

Nausea: I once prayed, "Dear God, please make me throw up every day if I must, but let me keep my hair." I lost my hair twice, but I never did get sick. Is that to say that I never felt nauseous? No, of course not. But even during bone marrow treatment my doctors were able to control it.

✺

Are you actually feeling sick or have you just formed an attachment to that pink and gray bucket? I was so sure that I would get sick that I kept that bucket at my side for days during BMT.

✺

A sign that should hang on every cancer patient's door: *Attention all visitors—no perfume or aftershave allowed!* That includes wearing the sweater you wore last night when you did have perfume on, thank you very much.

✺

Inside Tips:
- Check with your doctor, but I had better results when I began taking anti-nausea medication before chemo. Actually, I took it before, between, and after each treatment.

- If you feel the least bit sick, take something for nausea immediately—don't wait! It's easier to prevent it than to alleviate it.

- It's okay to let someone know if an aftershave, perfume, or anything else is bothering you.

- Some of your favorite foods may no longer seem appetizing. That's okay—try some new ones. (Hmm, I wonder if God purposely gave raw veggies no smell?)

- For me, when nothing else sounded good, tomato soup did. Don't laugh until you've tried it. Many patients have agreed with me once they tried it. Campbell's Italian Tomato was the best. I think the acidity helps.

- There are wonderful natural remedies for nausea too. Again, check with your doctor, but many patients have good results with ginger, licorice, or chamomile teas.

🌿

Mouth Sores: Some people get them, many don't. I followed the regimen recommended by my doctor and had no problems. If you do have problems, don't suffer silently. There are pain medications for this side effect.

🌿

Memory Lapses: New research has finally verified what cancer patients have known all along. Chemotherapy typically causes lapses in memory or concentration, more commonly known as "chemo brain."

For years, patients' complaints about chemo brain have been laughed off by some doctors, leaving the patients feeling as if we are crazy or that it's only happening to us. Hah! Now our doctors know the truth.

Is chemo brain something to fear? Of course not. It doesn't handicap you. You don't suddenly need name tags sewn in your clothes or anything. In general, the less chemo you have, the quicker the memory lapses recede. But to deny that it happens is insulting.

My experience with memory lapses was probably about as bad as it gets. I had twelve months of very aggressive chemotherapy, my lifetime limit of adriamycin, and then a bone marrow transplant! I still have some difficulty with memory and concentration, but it's probably more noticeable to me than to anyone around me.

❧

I used to hate functions where they made you put those sticky nametags on your clothes. Now I wish everyone wore one on their forehead.

❧

SIDE EFFECTS

When we try to explain chemo brain to you, don't tell us that you too forget where you've put your keys. Lord, I once forgot where I put my car!

✺

They say that this too shall pass, but I'm not sure if my memory will ever be quite as sharp as it was before treatment, but that's okay. Memory is overrated anyway; that's why we invented pens and paper.

✺

Final thought on Side Effects: I've pretty much done it all, so maybe this question sums it up best. If I had to do it all over again, side effects included, would I? You bet I would. All side effects are temporary, but wellness is something I plan on keeping for a long time.

✺

HAIR LOSS

I did all that was asked of me and I tried to do it well—treatment, therapy, bone marrow transplant—but I am not embarrassed, nor do I feel superficial, to admit that hair loss for me was a big issue.

I have seen the fear and disbelief in other patients' faces when they have come to the point in their treatment where they may lose their hair—and they ask me, with their searching eyes, "Did you lose yours?" There is a sense of embarrassment that a "little thing" like hair loss should even be a concern when we are fighting for our lives. It is often only when I admit that I too had difficulty with this that they feel free enough to openly discuss their own fears and difficulties in coming to terms with it.

Losing our hair hurts and no one tells us that. It hurts our head, yes, but mostly it hurts our heart.

It is "only" hair when it is someone else's!

No, losing your hair over decades is not the same thing!

❧

Never ask a cancer patient what is more important—
their hair or their life? We all know the answer to that
one, but I've yet to find anyone willing to sign a statement, "Lose your hair, gain your life." If that were the
case, we would get out the clippers ourselves.

❧

The fear of losing your hair, along with actually losing it,
is truly worse than having it gone. I would've never
believed it, but it is true.

❧

Yes, yes, yes, we've heard that it comes back better than
before, but you seem to be missing the point. In order
for it to come back better than before we first have to
lose it!

❧

The next person who carelessly says, "It's only hair," ask
them to share the experience of baldness with you.

❧

Wigs—to think I once wore one for fun.

❧

HAIR LOSS

A bad hair day takes on a whole new meaning.

✺

When I lost my hair, my eyelashes, my eyebrows, I felt as if I were being erased.

✺

Hair loss allows our illness to enter the room before our name.

✺

I once had a reporter ask me during a photo shoot if I would remove my wig for *impact*. Sure, I told her, right after I take off my bra and unbutton my pants so that you can see the lumpectomy and ovariectomy scars, too, for full effect. How dare she make that request. I was fighting for my life—*that* was the impact of the story!

✺

A nurse once asked me to stop in and see a patient who wasn't doing so well. There she lay, in the middle of July, with her bare head covered with a stocking cap. She was so depressed. She began to cry, not about the cancer, but about how she looked. She was a young mom with no money.

Well, when I had been fund-raising for my bone marrow transplant someone had sent me $100 for a wig that someone else had sent to her when she had needed it. I had hung onto that money, waiting for the right time. Here it was. I later received a smiling picture of the young mother with her 4-year-old sitting on her lap. The note said that, thanks to the new wig, her child was no longer afraid of her. Medicine can come in many forms; that wig was medicine for her heart, her spirit and my soul.

※

Rightfully mourn the loss of your hair as you would any other significant loss.

※

From my journal, written during my cancer treatment: *The process of losing my hair has begun—maybe the process of saving my life has, too.*

※

No one had a harder time losing their hair than I did—
yet I survived, as will you.

🌿

I just recently bought a small hairpiece for a party to
add to my hair. I guess I have come a long way!

🌿

Parting tips: Get a wig, before you lose your hair.
Don't just accept your wig as-is, have it professionally
cut and styled the way you want it. Yes, a wig is a
temporary thing, but if at all possible invest a little
extra money in this purchase. Get a great one—you're
worth it.

🌿

No matter how much we like our doctors, no matter how happy we would be to have them over to the house for dinner and include them as family, there is still something about stepping into that office that brings to mind the word, "dreaded."

※

I used to think when someone said, "She has ice water in her veins," it meant that she was hard, cold, and formidable. Now I know it merely meant she was standing outside the doctor's office doors trying to get her feet to carry her through.

※

I once worked for General Motors and had to get up at 4:30 A.M. My dad told me that I would get used to it. I never did; it was always a fight. I don't care how many times we go to the doctor—that, too, is never a walk in the park.

※

Check your modesty at the door with your clothes. Just keep telling yourself that he or she has seen thousands of *these* (whatever these are) before.

※

Write your questions and concerns down *before* you go to the doctor. There are no stupid questions or concerns. If you have been made to feel so, it's not your choice of question that is stupid—it may be your choice of doctor that needs examining.

Remember, your tumors didn't walk into that office alone. I once told a doctor that unless he could find a way for me to leave my tumors on the examining table while I went shopping, he had to treat all of me, that I was a package deal—mind, body, and soul.

❦

There is more to us than what is written on a chart or read in a test result.

❦

"How are you doing?" should mean more than "How are your tumors?" Wouldn't it be great to have a doctor ask about our heart and have it mean the place where we keep our feelings? Can't you just hear it: "How's your heart today? Any excess buildup of fears or worries we need to work on?"

❦

Often loved ones don't understand the fear and anxiety that begins a few days before tests and lasts right up until you talk to the doctor. The next time someone tries to blow it off by telling you that they know it will be okay (or if it's not, you can handle it), just say, "I'm glad you feel that way because I've scheduled some exploratory tests that you should have at the same time." After you've heard all their excuses as to why this isn't a good time for them, remind them that even someone who has always been healthy would worry if they were being examined as thoroughly as we are.

☙

Once, when I was getting ready to have all my scans run, someone actually said to me, "I can hardly wait until I am as far out as you so that I won't have to worry." If there is such a thing as that far out, I haven't yet reached it. I think as long as I'm still playing with a full deck, I'll worry at test times.

☙

Why can't they change the magazines?

☙

Paper gowns should be outlawed!

☙

"Oh, you have good juicy veins. Oops, I *thought* you had good juicy veins."

✻

"You won't feel a thing."

✻

I once heard syndicated newspaper columnist Linda Ellerbee speak. Like all of us, she said that she went into shock when she was first diagnosed with breast cancer. Later she called her doctor to set up another appointment because she had so many questions. Believe it or not, her doctor told her he didn't have time. He suggested that she go read some books, and then if she still had questions, he would answer them. She calmly told the doctor that the books were a good idea, but any future questions would be directed to any other doctor but him. Good girl!

✻

Personally, I've experienced both the best and worst-case scenarios. Let me leave you with the best, just to show you how it can be, should be. Yes, I still dread visiting the doctor's office for a test. Yes, I've even put it off (hard to believe, right?). But, in my case, a visit to

Cancer Treatment Centers of America is rather like
going home.

There's an old saying, "Home is where the heart is."
Well, they have big hearts at CTCA and they're not
afraid to show it. No matter what the outcome of the
tests, I know I can handle it because they'll be right
there, through thick and thin, to patiently and professionally help me. I am never "just another cancer
patient" to them—no one is. I never feel like I'm a
number or an inconvenience; I always feel like I'm family.

The founder of the hospital lost his mother to cancer
and he developed what they call the "mother standard."
Simply put, the goal is to treat everyone as if he or she
were your own mother lying in that bed. That's the kind
of care that you need to help you defeat cancer. If you
don't have it, then please look around until you get it.
You deserve it.

※

The right doctors and care providers do more than care for us, they care about us.

🌿

Dedicated oncologists and nurses *choose* to work, on a daily basis, in a role that most of us would avoid like the plague if we could. I thank God nightly for their positive form of insanity. For virtually no one is working in the field of cancer for the money; there are far easier ways of earning it.

🌿

One of my greatest gifts came when I finally found a doctor who told me that if I chose to fight he would fight with me and for me with everything at his disposal and anything he could find. The statistics be damned.

🌿

Good doctors don't just tell you what needs to be done; they make you believe that you can do it. I had the best.

🌿

The great ones understand that all the medication that we need can't be administered by others per orders on a chart or simply written on a prescription pad. They know that their healing comes to us, too, in the form of quality time spent with us, in the gentleness with which they relay information to us, in the encouragement they provide us, and in the bond of trust we build.

❧

I had the luxury of feeling safe with my doctors—not safe in terms of life and death, but safe as with a trusted friend or family member. Safe that they would do all that it took for me, and safe that they would help me do all that they asked.

❧

It is only by getting to know you that your doctor can truly decide if you need a good cry or a good stiff kick in the butt.

❧

The great nurses understand that when they answer a call button, it is not always our bodies that need their attention—they may find a mind that needs calming, a heart that needs soothing, or simply a hand that needs holding. A good hospital gives its nurses time to do so.

❧

The truly great ones sit on the bed sometimes.

❧

The truly great ones understand that illness intensifies the small child in all of us.

🌿

The truly great ones drop that shield of self-preservation, of distance, that often stands between them and us. They must pay an awfully high price for doing so, but God we love them for it.

🌿

Cancer patients aren't the only ones who need success stories. Doctors and nurses need success stories, too. After I successfully completed my bone marrow transplant I went back for a routine checkup. I made a point of dropping by the bone marrow unit. They told me that I was one of the few patients who had ever come back to personally say, "Thank you." I found that appalling.

🌿

The truly great ones hurt for us, and there are far more of "us" than them.

🌿

The truly great ones show us that we can believe in them, sometimes before we believe in ourselves.

🌿

THE TRULY GREAT ONES

During my treatment the truly great ones let me ride along on their hope for me until I could find my own.

✼

When I didn't fit into any of the existing treatment protocols, one of the truly great ones found a new protocol for me.

✼

Once, when I was trying to decide whether or not I would go through with bone marrow transplant, Doctor Sanchez came in to see why I was still debating. I told him I wasn't sure I could do it, that everything I had read was so horrible. He looked at me over those little half-glasses and said, "If I didn't know that you could do it, it wouldn't be an option." It wasn't arrogance, and I knew his decision wasn't based solely on any chart or test—it was based on me—the "me" he had taken the trouble to thoroughly get to know.

✼

One of the truly great ones once told me that he doesn't know how we patients keep doing what we do. I told him that we have no choice; frankly I don't know how he keeps doing what he does.

✼

EVERYDAY LIFE

"Everyday living requires courage," said Eleanor Roosevelt, "we must do the things we think we cannot do."

✵

It is not always the big things that get to us. In fact, the plain old everyday details of life in-between treatments can be the most difficult of all. I found the "in-between" to be the biggest breeding ground for fatigue, depression, worry, fear, and the "what ifs"—but it's also where fun, joy, laughter, and great love can abound. After all, the "in-between" is where we spend the largest part of our treatment. Here are some things we've all felt, along with some gentle reminders:

- Courage: *Sure wish there were brave pills.*
- Too bad life doesn't have hazardous duty pay.
- Too bad you can't bank happy days and use them as needed.
- What a phony I often am when I smile and say I'm fine. Oh well, it seems to make them happy. They accept it so readily.
- The wind is blowing. My wig is on. Is it straight, will it stay on, will this ever end?

It is perfectly okay to have a "poor me" day—and it is equally okay to let someone know about it. Call a friend and tell them right up front, "I am really feeling lousy today, and I called to see if you could help." You will be surprised what a lift this will give you. Your friend will make a conscious effort to cheer you, and you will have the luxury of being cared for in a special way. You will both hang up feeling better and closer. Remember to give as well as receive. Friends without cancer sometimes need cheering, too.

Often we must learn that we can be "well" without being cured.

Each and every day is a gift. Some presents are just better than others.

There is something good in every single day that we are given; sometimes we just have to look a little harder.

꽃

Before cancer, life just seemed to happen. During and since cancer, life seems more...more what? More acknowledged, more deliberate, more intense? Maybe just more.

꽃

Cancer causes us to think about life. It causes us to listen to the inside of us more than we may be used to. Neither of these is a bad thing.

꽃

Rest: While taking treatment I often felt like a wind-up clock. I said "wind-up," not "battery-operated." A battery-operated clock begins to lose seconds, then minutes, before it stops; but when a wind-up clock stops, it stops. It is natural to have very little reserve energy, to be going along fine one minute and be totally beat the next. Sit down, lie down, and let your clock rewind.

꽃

It's a myth to think that you are valuable only when you are active and busy.

🌿

Pick and choose your battles. Fighting fatigue is pointless. Take a nap.

🌿

I once felt that each time I rested I was giving in to the
cancer, that cancer was winning. Not true. Michael
Jordan, a supreme athlete, grabbed all the rest he could
during the NBA Playoffs—and we are in the biggest
playoff of our lives!

🌿

Even while resting, the battle inside your body is going
on, cell by cell. Sometimes just let the body rest so the
cells can concentrate on only one job at a time.

🌿

As important as it is to rest, it is also important to take
on a challenge here and there. There is such a thing as
"good fatigue"—the kind you get from doing something
constructive, even if it wipes you out for the rest of the
day. It is sometimes difficult for loved ones to understand this.

After my bone marrow transplant, I decided one day to clean house, change the bed, and cook dinner for Rick. Now, this was a lot to tackle at that time, and I couldn't have done it every day, and it did wipe me out. That night I was very tired, but it was such a good tired—not the kind of tired you get from having lain on the couch all day, but a tired as in, "I've accomplished something and it was worth it." The same can be said of a visit with a friend, or dinner and a movie. It is often when the body is active that the mind and heart rests.

※

Sometimes we must remember the wisdom of the old "half a loaf" rule. I was talking to a woman once who was very depressed. Prior to treatment she could work for hours at a time in her garden, but now she was tired after an hour or so. I reminded her not to allow the exasperation of her new limitations to destroy the wonder of the time she did have. After all, that single hour had been wonderful, had it not?

※

Refuse to get depressed about things that you can't do at this time; it doesn't mean that you won't do them ever again.

※

Worry: Don't waste today's strength and energy worrying about having enough strength and energy for tomorrow. Tomorrow will come with its own supply.

※

"Where will I be next year at this time?" is something we often ask ourselves during treatment. Maybe a better question is, "Where am I now, and how can I take full advantage of it?"

※

I have been nearsighted most of my life. I would prefer perfect vision, but if I have to be either nearsighted or farsighted, I'll take nearsighted. Let me focus on what is right in front of me and I'll deal with the rest when it gets here.

※

Shut some doors: Here's a little visualization technique that really helped me. Think of your mind as a big house, and today is cleaning day. Put your cancer decisions, treatment worries, etc. in one room, your work demands in another, your family and friends in yet another. Each of these rooms has a large heavy door that you can close tightly. Don't feel the need to drag all the cancer stuff into each room with you all the time.

Shutting the "cancer" door now and then doesn't mean you are avoiding the problems or decisions. It is rather like shutting the door to a teenager's bedroom; the mess doesn't disappear, but at least you don't have to look at it for a while.

When we stop to realize just how many worries and problems we have been "mind dragging" around with us—it's no wonder we feel tired, stressed, and overwhelmed. Shut some doors!

❦

Before cancer I never considered my everyday thoughts as something I needed to do battle with, rage at, fight for control over, or learn to master. A thought simply "was." I now know that we can alter, we can rein in, we can lead our thoughts to a better place than they may automatically choose to go. We can actually train our everyday thoughts to be our biggest allies and work for us, not against us.

❦

Pets: Research on pets and pet lovers confirms what many of us already knew. Pets can reduce your blood pressure and heart rate, relieve anxiety and stress. During treatment, when my cat Misty would curl up with me, I just felt better. She seemed to sense when I was down and I responded to her nearness. Petting her seemed, for a time, to put the world in balance again. Simply put, I loved her and she loved me, which is always a good thing. If you have a pet, I don't have to explain any of this; if you don't, you really don't know what you are missing. Maybe this is a good time to find out.

❧

E-mail: Believe it or not, I just started e-mailing, but a friend of mine swore by her "cyber mail" when she was fighting cancer. She said that she got to talk to friends, loved ones, and new acquaintances all over the world—and it was her choice to let them know whether or not she had cancer. She was a crafter, and she said she found it freeing to talk "normally" to people online without their asking how she was or worrying about her. She could also stay in touch with other cancer patients, day or night.

❧

Here is advice that should be written on a prescription pad. If you are feeling sad and blue—shut off the TV and pick up the telephone (or keyboard, if you have e-mail). Reach out and touch a living breathing person who can respond to you. We all need interaction. When other people enter the room, the ghosts and goblins may not totally disappear, but they sure get harder to hear.

🌿

Remember what you are fighting for. Stop every once in a while during your struggles to remind yourself just why you are fighting, why you want to stay around a while longer. Chances are, it's not to climb Mount Everest or to swim the English Channel. My guess is that much simpler and far more important things are on your mind—and the good news is that cancer can't stop you from doing most of those things, right now. Today, for example, spend time with your loved ones. Make cookies or go fishing with a child or grandchild. Hold hands, take a walk, sit and talk with someone special. These are the things you are fighting for, and cancer can't stop you from enjoying these pleasures—only you can stop yourself.

🌿

During treatment it's the easiest thing in the world to just throw away time. The little tape recorder in our head constantly says, "Boy, I can hardly wait for the next month, or three months, or six months to be over— because then I am finished with treatment and I can start living again." *Whoa!* Isn't the whole reason that we are doing treatment to gain more time? Maybe we should stop and revel in the time that we have right now, instead of wishing it away.

✿

Again, remember what you are fighting for. You are fighting for more days. Today you have one. Find a way of enjoying it.

✿

I've heard people say, time and again, "I'm not doing this very well." Hey, the point is, you are doing it! The "well" part will come and go.

✿

Guilt: Don't accept the guilt for your illness. I have a real problem with books that tell us that we somehow "thought" ourselves sick, that we worried or stressed ourselves into cancer, or that some difficulty in our lives somehow brought on our illness. Some even suggest that a spouse can say things to endanger us—or that things totally beyond our control such as the loss of a loved one, or a stressful job cause cancer. I refuse to accept this. No one is exempt from tragedy and, yet, not everyone gets cancer.

✿

I refuse to think of my loved ones as potential "cancer bombs." Many times I have had a patient or former patient come to me in tears, their fear in high gear over this issue. They are terrified because they have had a fight with their spouse, or a parent has died. One woman actually asked me which would be more damaging to her—to stay in a difficult marriage, or to get a divorce—for she had read that both will cause cancer. I heard one woman, while fighting with her spouse, actually accuse him of *causing* her cancer. The look on his face was heartbreaking, as was her statement.

※

I have found that when people tell us that our lives are too stressful, they often mean that our lives would be too stressful for *them*. They don't consider that living our lives like theirs would be stressful for us. That's why God made us all different. For me, being surrounded by family and kids is not stressful, even with all the noise, commotion, and problems that accompany it. Stress to me would be sitting quietly in a fishing boat.

※

Some books tell us that even *good* stress is bad for us. Guess we really didn't want that new baby, new house, or new job we have worked for. Challenge and stress are not the same things. If we must eliminate the bad stress *and* the good stress from our lives, what is left? Doesn't matter because we can't—it's called life.

🌿

So, at the bottom line, what is my humble opinion? Concentrate on the stresses that bother you and try to *reduce* those in your life, certainly. Take care of yourself, eat healthy, and do all that you can to regain or retain good mental health, but don't add to the heavy burden you are already carrying by feeling that you brought this illness on yourself with your thoughts or your feelings. Or that your thoughts or feelings will accelerate it. That's enough to *really* stress you out!

🌿

I was once home alone and feeling blue, and rare tears began to flow with tiredness and "what ifs." I immediately thought, "No! Don't think that way. You are going to make yourself sicker. You must think positive!" What terrible pressure to put on yourself—to always be positive, to always be up. An occasional negative thought or fear will *not* jeopardize your care. Even the most positive and successful patients have entertained some doubts at times.

🌿

EVERYDAY LIFE

During treatment I realized that it wasn't so important
to have a perfectly clean house. I found that the fingerprints of little ones on glass could be charming, and that
toilet bowls continue to function even if they are not
scrubbed every week.

≭

Tomorrow is always another day, a new beginning. This
is a good thing. Do not play "carry-over" by dragging
today's doubts or troubles into tomorrow. Stop telling
yourself, "Oh, tomorrow is just another day like today."
Hey, tomorrow hasn't even been born yet! It will arrive,
fresh and new and full of seconds, minutes, and hours—
all waiting for you to inscribe your life upon them. If
today was rough, rest up, clear your mind, and get ready
to start fresh tomorrow. Time is your ally, not your
enemy.

Yes, I realize that everyone experiences nighttime every 24 hours, but not with the same intensity or restlessness as cancer patients. Nighttime blues or frights are a very common and understandable side effect of the illness and treatment. Again, I write the following to let you know that you are not alone in this.

❦

Years ago, a dear friend returned from Vietnam after losing both legs. The night he returned he and I sat up talking throughout a long summer's night. At one point we were both quietly looking at the stars and he commented, "How loud the quiet is." I thought I understood. I now know that until I had cancer I never really had. It is in the loudness of the midnight silences that either your hope or your despair is most often heard.

❦

What was God thinking? Why does everything hurt more at night, fevers run higher at night, sounds seem scarier at night, hours seem longer at night, worries seem more abundant and larger at night—and this is when He meant for us to sleep?!

❦

I'll lay real still and not open my eyes. Please, sleep, re-claim me and take me back to the peace of nothingness.

꙰

Am I the only one in the whole world awake? With my thoughts screaming like this, how could anyone around me possibly be asleep?

꙰

If I am fighting so hard to live, why do I yearn so deeply for the sweet nothing of sleep?

꙰

How sad, I used to love the night—the peace, the quiet coziness. Now the edges are too sharp and the phantoms seem closer in the dark.

꙰

Where is the OFF SWITCH?

꙰

Audio Books: Here's one of the ways I learned to deal with the nighttime blues. During treatment, I decided that I would look at any period of forced inactivity as a mini-vacation. Since I love to read, I thought I would just curl up with a good book and read the time away. The theory sounds good, but the reality is far different. I couldn't concentrate. What did I just read? Why is it taking so long to read this page? It was at this time that my husband brought me my first audio books. What a treasure! With headphones, the narrator's voice could often override my own meandering thoughts. If you don't like the first audio book, keep trying until you find a narrator you like. My audio books were a godsend, especially at night.

Other Tips:

- If you really can't sleep, get up and do something; don't just lie there and fret.

- If things are really bothering you, turn on the light; nothing is as bad in the light.

- Remember, things really do look different in the morning, and morning *will* come.

- In support groups or in cancer chat rooms you can often find a night-time cancer friend—believe me, you are not the only one awake!

🌿

Just ask! If you are consistently having a problem sleeping, ask for something. If you are having anxiety attacks or nervousness, ask for something. It is not a sign of weakness to admit that we sometimes need help—it is a sign of strength. Often we think, "Well, it's not that bad." Well, how bad does it have to be? Remember to change the things you can; there are enough things that you can't.

🌿

OUR CHILDREN

I have no biological children. Rick and I were trying to get pregnant when I was diagnosed with cancer. Because of this, I am extremely close to my nieces and nephews. Still, I know that nothing quite compares with the way cancer tears at the hearts of a parent and child. Having spoken to literally thousands of cancer patients over the years, here are some things I've learned from the parents and their kids.

⁂

Kids are smarter than we think. (Jeez, Vickie, no kidding.) I know, I know…we say this all the time, but we obviously forget it or we wouldn't try to hide so much from them. Parents sometimes try to keep cancer a secret in the home because they don't want their kids to worry. I understand your motives, but do you actually think your children are not going to pick up on the fact that *something* is wrong? Please don't let cancer be the big pink elephant in your living room that everyone is pretending isn't there. Trust me, your children will find out—so, please, let the news come from you.

⁂

I've seen situations where parents were trying to keep it from their kids only to have the kids find out at school—and then, in turn, the kids tried to conceal from their parents that they knew. The whole family was in silent chaos, with no one comforting each other.

※

Left in a vacuum, a child's imagination, like our own, can conjure up frightening images and worries that are often far worse than the situation warrants.

※

When you tell your children, have a clearly conceived game plan in place and share it. Yes, Mom or Dad has cancer and this is exactly what we intend to do about it. If you want them to feel confident and positive, then show them that *you* are.

※

Address the issue of death right up front. If your child is old enough to go to school, he or she has probably heard of someone dying of cancer. Even the *possibility* of losing a parent is terrifying. I've talked to kids whose mom had Stage One breast cancer, very curable, but because it was cancer, the kids were terrified that she was going to die. Of course they would not say so to her, so they worried needlessly for months. When I say address death, it need not be, "I'm not going to die," but it can be, "We're going to be okay."

※

A cancer patient complained to me that her 13-year-old was acting up. "This is such a difficult time, you would think my daughter would be on her best behavior," she said. Well, it doesn't always work that way—not with kids, friends, spouses, or family. When asked, the 13-year-old clearly explained the problem. Yes, her mom had told her that she had cancer, but there had been no subsequent updates or discussions. She said the neighbors knew more about her mother's treatment, setbacks, and progress than she did. Once her mom started to include her more, even ask for her help around the house, things got better.

※

If we are all in this together, let's not leave them out.

※

Sometimes kids are just plain mad. You wonder, "Gee, is my child mad at *me*, or mad at the cancer?" It doesn't really matter; don't take it personally. Sometimes "mad" is just a whole lot easier for kids than "scared."

※

OUR CHILDREN

If only we knew what goes on in a child's heart and mind. For example, when my little niece Chelsea's maternal grandmother was battling cancer, Chelsea did everything she could to help. She waited hand-and-foot on her grandmother, comforting her with frequent hugs and kisses. Her mother noticed that Chelsea was also ducking frequently into the bathroom to wash her hands.

One night, as her mom was tucking her in bed, Chelsea finally asked if cancer was "catching." God love her! With so much cancer all around us, any child might assume it was contagious. But did the fear of catching cancer stop my little niece from giving her grandma all those hugs and kisses? No, all she could do was bravely wash her hands and continue to love Grandma. I wonder if any adult would have been so courageous.

🌿

Kids have long antennae. They pick up so much. My little nephew, Zachary, once asked if I was "broken bad?"

🌿

The gentleness of children: My sisters and I had gone up north to visit my brother and his family. We went into town to do a little shopping. We were crossing the street when my little niece Mallory, then about six, reached up and took my hand. She said, "Be careful,

Aunt Vickie, you can't get hit by a car because you have cancer."

❦

A mother who was recuperating from cancer surgery didn't have to cook dinner for a while. Each night a different friend or relative would bring a wonderful meal. One night it was roast beef, mashed potatoes and gravy—the works. When they all sat down to eat, her son suddenly bolted from the table in tears. She found him on her bed, a sure sign that he wanted to talk. All he could say was that he just wanted macaroni and cheese and hot dogs again. What he was *really* saying was that he just wanted things back to normal. Luckily for him, his mom understood what he couldn't say.

❦

We use every opportunity to teach our children different lessons. Is there anyone out there who hasn't climbed the stairs, holding a little one's hand, counting each and every step? As the children grow, the lessons grow. "What color is this ball? How much change do you get back from this dollar?" And so it goes.

Cancer, or any other illness, provides an incredible opportunity to teach our children some priceless lessons, and to do it the best way possible—by example. Show them what it means to be brave in the face of difficulties; let them see you accomplishing tasks that you would rather not do at all. Teach them that it is okay to be sad sometimes, but that "sad" doesn't mean "defeated." Each of us, including your own children, will experience difficulties at some point in life. The way in which you handle your battles can provide them with a gleaming suit of armor for theirs: "If my mom or dad, or my grandmother or grandfather could do *that*, I can certainly do *this*."

※

You are a better hero, by far, than any TV wrestler.

※

I don't believe that heroes are extraordinary people— I believe they are ordinary people in extraordinary circumstances. This is a wonderful lesson for adults and children. Not all heroes wear capes!

※

We do all that we can to protect our kids. We get them inoculated for everything from whooping cough to measles. We teach them to look both ways before they cross the street. We teach them to go to the dentist every six months. Now I don't know what the odds are of dying from measles, a cavity, or even an auto accident, but I do know that one in eight of our daughters will at some point face breast cancer. Are we teaching them about breast self-exams? With a bra comes responsibility. By teaching your daughter BSE, you're giving her a tool that may someday save her life.

※

Ask your kids for help. They love feeling needed and useful. Don't we all?

※

Set up a "special buddy" for your child during this time. It could be an aunt, uncle, or an adult friend—someone other than mom or dad. Have this special friend arrange some time alone with the child so they can talk freely about what is going on. Let the child know that he or she can call on their special friend whenever they need to—or ask any questions that they would rather not ask mom or dad. I know a 10-year-old boy who was given a business card with his special friend's phone numbers on it—cell phone, pager, home, and work numbers. It brought a lump to my throat one day as I watched this little guy carefully pull this tattered "buddy card" from his pocket.

※

Oh yes, and be sure to tell your child's school what is going on!

※

I'll let you in on a little secret. Sometimes we do want to talk about it.

※

When cancer patients voice a problem or concern, you are mistaken if you think that we always want you to try to cheer us up. Or that we expect you to fix us. We don't. Sometimes we just need to voice our frustration at the viciousness of this disease.

※

Then again, cancer is not the "only" thing we want to talk about. We still enjoy a good joke or a little gossip. As much as family and friends love us, even *they* can only take us in small doses. Well, we too need a break from being us.

※

Those of you who love us—please, never be so afraid of our tears that you won't let us cry with you. For if you never see us cry, believe me it doesn't mean we aren't crying. It only means we're doing it alone.

※

OH, HOW MISTAKEN YOU ARE!

You would let me cry if I wrecked the car, or if my dog died, or if I fought with my spouse. Why won't you let me cry a little when I have cancer?

❧

Another misconception: "I bet this has brought the two of you so close together."

❧

All interpersonal dynamics change with this disease. Before cancer, you could complain at work about a husband who refused to pick up his clothes, and friends would agree that they had one, too. Now it's, "How could he treat her that way—she has cancer!"

❧

Before cancer he could complain that she never fills the gas tank, and his friends would agree. Now it's, "How could he expect her to fill the tank—she has cancer!"

❧

Life continues, folks. There are very few clear-cut heroes or villains—only everyday people doing their best in extremely difficult circumstances.

❧

Try to understand that we do have other concerns besides survival. My cancer was estrogen positive. The

OH, HOW MISTAKEN YOU ARE!

day that I received my first terminal diagnosis it was decided that my ovaries would be removed as part of my treatment. I knew this was necessary to extend my life, but I had never had children. Now I'm not stupid; I knew that a terminal diagnosis had seriously jeopardized my entire future, let alone my chance for children. Still, the removal of my ovaries was so difficult and so final.

The point of my story is that no one—not one person—stopped to talk to me about this. I understand that saving my life was the more immediate concern. But I cried long and late into my pillow the night before surgery—not because of the surgery, but because I now knew that no one would ever call me mommy, there would be no first days of school, or teeth for the tooth fairy. By morning, the chance for any of that would be gone forever. I silently cried for my broken heart. Fear for my life that night was way down the line.

❧

Try to understand the need for us to continue as many of the fun things in life as possible. Bite back the ever-present, "Don't tire yourself," or "That's just going to wear you out." Please don't take away all the things that we are fighting for!

❧

OH, HOW MISTAKEN YOU ARE!

Sales people, waitresses, taxi drivers, fellow employees, strangers on the street—just because you see a bald head or sell us a cancer book or have heard through the grapevine that we have cancer, please understand that we are not in mourning. Smile and laugh with us, and chances are we'll laugh right back.

🌾

I once had a friend named Joy. She was the first "cancer friend" I met. We were taking treatment together. She was a wonderful, upbeat person, always so sure of herself, always so positive. She would come into my room and ask how I was and I would tell her "fine, doing great"—just as she assured me that she was. When she would leave, I would wonder what she would think of me if she knew how I really felt.

Then one day I walked in and caught her crying. We were honest that day and I found out that she, too, had doubts. I realized that, just as I had been "fine" and "okay" when she asked, she, too, had been saying the same brave things to me. We had each been left with the impression that we weren't as brave as the other. How sad that we had wasted time in which we could have been helping each other.

🌾

Even if we "look good" during treatment, it doesn't necessarily mean that the treatment itself is a piece of cake. I hear this complaint from patients all the time, and I understand exactly what they mean. People come up to them and flippantly say, "Well, you must be feeling good because you sure look great," or "You look too good to be sick." Although meant as a compliment, such statements tend to undercut all the effort and determination that it now takes to simply look "normal." If you want to pay us a compliment, please recognize and validate our struggle. Try this: "With everything you are going through, I don't know how you manage to look so good."

🌿

What you don't see: There are certain kinds of pain (I am not talking physical pain here, I'm talking flat-out, bone-tired-of-it-all pain) that isn't accompanied by blood and therefore goes unnoticed. Just because you can't "see" the pain in us, that doesn't mean we aren't feeling it.

For example, during treatment I always wore my wig. I think only two people ever saw me without it, and then only for a second. I wore pretty nightgowns and cute PJs. I went to *exhausting* lengths to appear as normal as possible. (Looking back, maybe I was just trying not to lose Vickie in all the treatment.) Based on my so-called "normal" appearance, many people suggested that I was somehow sailing through breast-to-bone cancer and treatment. They also assumed that I didn't need as much support as others. Believe me, no one "sails" through these treatments. To even suggest such a thing is so demoralizing to the patient. Must the blood be visible before anyone realizes that we are hurting?

❦

The most difficult aspect of cancer is the physical pain? Wrong, wrong, wrong!

❦

"What ifs" are natural parts of the cancer battle. We say it silently in our head and our heart much more often than we say it aloud. When an occasional "what if" slips out, please don't tell us not to say such a thing. Reality has been forced upon us—please occasionally just let us share it openly with you.

❦

If our cancer is anything other than Stage One, few patients find it comforting when the average person steps up and assures them that they will be all right. Sorry, but that can actually come off as rather insulting. You don't know, nor do we yet. Your, "Oh, don't worry, you'll be just fine," brings no comfort because you really have no basis for saying so, and it minimizes the concerns and fears that we are living with every day. It is better to say, "You'll get through this."

🌿

On the other hand, don't think that you can't share a good cancer success story with us. Believe me, we feed on others' successes. Here are two basic rules of thumb as to whether or not to share the story: One, it must have a successful outcome (you would think that goes without saying—it doesn't); and two, the star of the story has to have had a type of cancer that is at least as bad, preferably worse, than ours. As happy as I was for them, I couldn't find much hope for myself (Stage Four and terminal) in the recovery stories of Stage One breast cancer patients.

🌿

Gifts: Often the best gifts we receive aren't wrapped in pretty paper with bright and shiny bows. They come in the form of meals cooked or casseroles delivered. Or someone who comes in and says, "Where is the laundry or the vacuum?" These are gifts of love and mean much more than a store-bought sweater. I once had a toilet scrubbed and nothing could have been much better.

🌿

Any card or letter that meets us at the mailbox leaves us with a smile.

🌿

SOMEONE ONCE SAID
(No kidding!)

"Do you ever worry about dying?"

✿

"Is that a wig?"

✿

"Don't you just love wearing wigs, I think it would be
fun." (Yeah, well, then wear one.)

✿

"I knew someone who had what you have, but she died."

✿

"Don't you ever get scared?"

✿

We hear this one all the time and, believe me, cancer
patients truly hate this statement: "Well, no one knows
how long they have. After all, I could walk outside right
now and get hit by a car." What? Did cancer patients
suddenly become car-immune? This is not a fair analogy.
Now, if you were being forced to walk blindfolded down
the middle of the expressway during rush hour—maybe
then we could talk.

✿

A friend once commented after complaining about her own marriage, "Well, at least the two of you now know what is important—I'm sure you never argue." Yeah, right.

I have found that illness, particularly long-term illness, intensifies everything. This is not always a good thing when feelings are so raw. Spouses living constantly in such intense situations do argue, and it often hurts even more than before. Of course, there are good times as well—times filled with the deepest love, friendship, and affection—and those too are usually more intense than before.

✼

Believe it or not…right after finding five spots of cancer on my bone scans a radiologist said to me, "Do you know what I would do if I were you?"

When I could breathe again, I asked him, "What?", thinking he was going to suggest a particular doctor or hospital.

He said, "I would stop at the first video store and rent all the Three Stooges movies I could find. They say that laughter is pretty much the best and only medicine for what you have." I think I could have murdered him on the spot and no jury would have convicted me.

✼

I had lots of blood transfusions after my bone marrow transplant because I wasn't producing enough reds or platelets. I had more than one person tell me they would really rather not have transfusions—"Don't you worry about AIDS?" No thank you, only one major illness worry at a time, please. Without those transfusions I wouldn't have had to worry about anything.

🌿

I had recently been diagnosed with terminal breast-to-bone cancer and been given only months to live. I was put on a potent type of high-dose pain medication and someone said, "Jeez, you want to be real careful of that stuff—you know, it can be habit forming." At the time I was more worried about the habit I already had—*living*.

🌿

"Do you ever worry about it coming back?"

🌿

"We changed the flavor of the barium. This one is good."

🌿

Zachary once asked me why God didn't make vegetables taste like chocolate, and chocolate taste like vegetables? Now *that* is a good question.

🌿

LOVED ONES MAKE AN
INCREDIBLE DIFFERENCE

Those of you who love us, we know there are times when you feel helpless. Please know that you never are, for your very presence brings us strength, and your love gives us our reason to fight.

🌾

No names, but you will recognize yourselves:

- You helped to place, to keep, and to guide my footsteps towards wellness.
- You came when my hair left.
- You sat with me on a bathroom floor and held me while I fell apart. We didn't even talk much. You didn't give me empty, "It will be okay's"— thank you for that. You just held me. Then you helped me pick up the pieces with a gentleness I will never forget.
- You always drove.
- You came because I *sounded* like I needed you.
- When I forgot why I was fighting, you reminded me.
- Once during raging fevers I asked you to tell me something good because I couldn't remember *anything* good—and you took me on a mental trip to Copper Harbor that I will never forget.

- You offered to cut your hair.
- You not only let me cry—you cried with me.
- You dedicated and donated your bridal dance to pay for my fight.
- You stopped to rest and said *you* were tired.
- You stood between the world and me.
- You called me every day.
- You took the time to write me a personal letter instead of calling. This enabled me to revisit your love and encouragement whenever I needed it. I still have it.
- When you had to fill my job, you called to reassure me that the replacement was only temporary.
- Mixed in with the bills that I had carried back to the hospital to pay, you slipped in a check. You did this at a time when you yourselves were paying for college and eating more macaroni and cheese than anybody should ever have to.
- You offered to refinance your house to pay for my fight. My God, what an offer!
- We held a benefit, and you all came.
- You sold more raffle tickets than I ever thought possible.

- Your restaurant became "free food" for my benefit.
- You both came to the hospital to be with us for my first test results—how brave, how loving.

🌿

When I had my bone marrow transplant, my whole family came down to be with Rick and me for the critical first week or so. The support meant more than I can ever say. I know there was a great deal of expense involved, but no one ever mentioned money. I will never be able to repay them for being my cheerleading squad, my support, my inspiration—my family. Their presence made the battle easier, their love made the battle worth it.

🌿

It has been said that the greatest gift that can be given is to lay down one's life for another. Well, many of our loved ones' lives have been laid down, put on hold, and set aside as we fight for ours. It is truly a gift beyond measure.

🌿

You walk through the darkness with us, not because you are ill and have to, but because you choose to. We were drafted, but you enlisted. We recognize and appreciate the difference more than words can ever say. YOU are our heroes, our support, and our reasons for fighting.

🌾

To love a cancer patient is, in turn, to feel sad, frightened, concerned, angry, lost, and often helpless—and to do all this, for the most part, silently. Does it help you, our Loved Ones, to know that we understand this? Believe me, we do recognize and deeply appreciate the incredibly high price you pay for loving us. Every victory is yours as much as ours.

🌾

POSITIVITY

Some people call it a "positive mental attitude," but that's not good enough. Yes, you need a positive attitude to defeat cancer, but you can't just sit around and "visualize" your way to wellness with positive thoughts. I think it's important that we connect our positive attitude to forward-moving action or activity. So, as a reminder, I've combined the word "positive" with the word "activity" and called it "positivity."

※

Positivity means that you are not just a dreamer—you are a doer. You don't just see yourself as a hopeful, passive, well-mannered, optimistic patient—you see yourself as a hopeful, proactive, well-educated, empowered cancer fighter.

※

We don't always get to choose which obstacles we face in life, but from the moment we were given free will it has always been our choice in *how* we deal with them. That's what positivity is all about.

※

To me, positivity is like learning to ride a bike. When the training wheels first came off, we all fell and skinned our knees. Now it was perfectly all right to cry for a minute about the blood running down our leg. It didn't mean that we wouldn't get back on the bike and learn to ride like the wind. It just meant that we were momentarily sad about the skin we had left on the pavement.

🌿

Does being positive mean that you never feel negative? Not at all! In fact, a cancer patient's second most-hated statement (behind, "it's only hair") is, "Now, Honey, you know it's important to stay positive." Or, "Don't think like that—remember, you have to be positive!" Well, take it from me—anyone who is positive 24/7 with cancer doesn't have both oars in the water.

🌿

In a perfect world we would all go around thinking only "happy thoughts" as Pollyanna did, but in a perfect world there would be no cancer.

🌿

Think of the first book you ever read on positive thinking. It was most likely, "The Little Engine That Could." Even he was allowed to say, "I think I can, I think I can." Not, "I can, I can, I can."

🌿

POSITIVITY

When I was little, I couldn't swallow pills, so my mom would mash them up and put them in something. Well, think of that mashed-up pill as your cancer treatment, and think of that "something" as positivity. Take your cancer treatment in mind-sized bites of positive thinking.

꽃

Whether you choose to think positive or negative, your mind is very powerful. The first time my little nephew, Zachary, had his blood drawn I was the one who took him to the doctor. He was very frightened. "I can't do this, I can't do this," he cried and—sure enough—there was no way he could get himself to do it. I knew he was scared because he had never done it before, but I assured him that he certainly *could* do it. We talked about it being just a little "pin prick" and all of that, but nothing worked. Finally, I encouraged him to say, "I can do this, I can do this, I can do this." It was amazing to watch. The more he said it, the more he believed it, and the more his confidence grew.

Remember, your heart is eavesdropping all the time on your thoughts. Zachary made it through the blood draw just fine, and he even watched. His next question reminded me of fears that we, too, sometimes have of things that will never happen. He said, "That wasn't bad at all. Does it hurt more when they put it back?"

꽃

POSITIVITY

Despite our best efforts to maintain an optimistic outlook, there are days when every cancer patient gets so discouraged about all the negative junk in our lives that we can no longer see the good. While this is normal, let's not wallow too long. On days like this, try making a negative/positive mind list. For every negative, think of a positive thing in your life that you wouldn't trade for the world. Chances are you will run out of negative things first.

✺

A man once called me and said that he had heard that I had a good positive attitude towards cancer and he wondered if I could talk to his wife. He said that her battle with the disease was really going quite well, but that she was having a problem staying "up." He said that he didn't want me to get the wrong idea. "It's not that she's a negative person," he said, "it's just that—well, let me put it this way—if she woke up on Christmas morning and found a pile of manure under the tree she is not the type of person who would automatically look for a pony."

When I stopped laughing, I told him that I'm not sure I would automatically look for the pony either. I have used this story many times over the past few years. When dealing with cancer, I always say, "Let us first admit that we have found a pile of manure under our Christmas tree. Let us occasionally gripe about the mess and the aroma—and then, and only then, will we not only *find* the pony, but we will learn to ride it."

🌿

Fighting cancer is like a giant game of "Mother May I." It sometimes seems as if we take one step forward only to take two steps back. Setbacks are a definite part of the battle. Just remember, it is not the speed of the game that counts. Treat all setbacks as temporary, rebound as quickly as possible, learn whatever you can from the particular experience, and then move forward again.

🌿

Isn't it funny how we only say, "Why me?" when something bad comes into our lives? We could just as easily turn it around. Each day, we could stop to look at all the good that God has brought us, and we could ask, "Why me?" Then say a silent prayer of thanks.

🌿

Negative thoughts can fuel our fears like oxygen feeds a fire. There are days when every inhale seems to add chaos and panic to our hearts and minds. A common calming technique is to take a deep breath and then exhale. There's logic to this, but at times I wanted to take *nothing* more in—there just was no more room. Sometimes I found it good to just concentrate on breathing out. With each exhale imagine that you are ridding yourself of bad thoughts, feelings, and fears. Yes, sometimes it is the "out" that matters more. Think of it as "mind cleaning"—you are just making room for better thoughts.

❦

I know there are days during treatment when you just feel empty. It's almost like you have felt every emotion a million times before and you can't seem to get enthused about anything—good or bad. You wonder if you are "all used up." Trust me, you may be temporarily dormant, but you're not used up. Just as everything beautiful in nature needs times of dormancy to leaf out, blossom, and bloom again, so, my friend, do you. Your colors (your feelings) will return. You could no more stop it from happening than a tree can stop its leaves from sprouting in spring. So, for a time, just rest. Trust me, you'll rebound.

❦

Forrest Gump said that life is like a box of chocolates. I couldn't agree more. I always hated the creamy centers, and sure enough I would get one. Now that doesn't mean that the whole box was bad. I just chewed through the cream as quickly as possible so that I could move on, hopefully, to a nut or a caramel. Despite cancer, I know that there are still lots of wonderful caramels and nuts in life.

❦

Who knows what you're *really* capable of? Nobody can teach you how to be you. Nobody could teach me how to be me. Nobody could tell me how far I could go. Nobody could tell me how much I could take. Nobody could tell me when enough was enough, because nobody knew but me—and I had to learn it myself. Before facing cancer and all the problems that it brought I was sure that there were certain problems that were too big for me or any one person. Today I believe that each of us can alter virtually anything that comes our way. You and I are capable of amazing things, if we just set our minds to it.

❦

Positivity can be as simple as deciding what to wear tomorrow.

❦

Positivity is making reservations.

❦

POSITIVITY

Cancer teaches us that living is a verb. It is an action word. Living is seeing, doing, feeling, saying, touching, smelling, tasting. It is climbing and it is occasionally falling. It is *not* a waiting word. Don't wait to live until you have accomplished a desired outcome. Starting right now, grab every minute of living out of each and every day.

❦

Humor is a big part of positivity, and it's one of our greatest weapons. On my way into surgery to have my ovaries removed, I made the surgeon (and myself) laugh when I asked her to do a bikini cut. I said that it would be a shame to waste this recent weight loss and, regardless of the outcome of my treatment, I still had at *least* one summer left in me.

❦

Cancer isn't contagious, but attitudes are. When I first had a CAT Scan at Cancer Treatment Centers of America, I discovered that a previous patient had secretly pasted some bright little dolphin stickers inside the scan. I loved it. Those little dolphins gave me something to think about besides the test.

Then CTCA got a new CAT Scan, and the powers that be weren't so sure about my covering the inside with stickers. I let it go for quite a while, but then I happened to run across the stickers: *Hang in there!* (with a turtle hanging on a rope)...*You're a Star!...Here's a Bear Hug! ...Smile!...You can make it!... Love, Vickie.* So I went down, waited until the room was empty, and completed my mission.

Well, you can't believe how many phone calls I got about the new stickers in the CAT scan. The one I appreciated the most said simply, "You really do understand, don't you?" Yes, yes, I understand, I remember, and my own heart still skips a beat when it's my turn in the scan.

❦

When I was first taking treatment there were eight of us—four patients and our spouses—who hung out together and got very close: Barbara and George, David and Pat, Joy and Paul, Rick and me. Oh, we definitely had an attitude; in fact, the doctors and nurses affectionately called us "The Brat Pack." We pushed our poles together, joined each other on the sun porch, sent our spouses out for an occasional unauthorized snack, watched TV, played games, did puzzles, and grew to love each other. We went to each other first to share our triumphs—and consoled each other through the losses.

Those three patients and their spouses taught me, the new kid on the block, so much about love, positivity, and dealing with this disease. Our cancers were very aggressive and in the late stages—so, yes, they taught me about friendship, about patience, and eventually they taught me about loss.

I have long since become the senior, the one who won't go away even in my wellness. Maybe Barbara, David, and Joy are partly to blame, for they taught me the importance of having someone hold a candle in the darkness and of inviting me to walk along. Now, whenever I hold a candle for someone new and frightened, they may not realize why my light is so bright, but I do. It's because Barbara, David, and Joy all left a piece of their light with me.

※

Every cancer patient feels guilty at times over the sadness and hardship that cancer is causing their family and friends. I know I did. Just keep in mind that it is the cancer that is causing the problems—not you.

※

It is sometimes hard to believe that this is all worth it to those who love us. That's the time to turn it around in your head and heart. If someone you loved were battling this disease, would you not *know* that it was worth every second of the struggle? Absolutely, so give them credit for loving *you* as deeply as you love them.

※

On breast and prostate cancer: Remember that a woman's femininity—who she is as a woman—has nothing to do with her cup size or whether there is anything in her cup at all. Same with prostate cancer. Even though they know better, some men naturally feel that their identity or masculinity is somehow linked to their prostate gland. Let's get something straight. None of us, whether male or female, is defined by any body part. Cancer is not a male or female issue—cancer is a human issue.

※

It's easy for you to identify the things in your life that are making you unhappy and worried. Now spend some time pinpointing what makes you happy, what makes you smile. Set aside time every day to dwell on these thoughts, too.

※

Life, any life, is a series of happenings and events—some good, some bad. Look at it this way: By fighting cancer, you're moving one of the bad ones into the past column of your life and getting ready for some of the good.

🌿

Think positive whenever you can. When you can't, call someone and have him or her do it for you.

🌿

I once looked up "support" in the dictionary. It says: "To carry the weight; To maintain position so as to keep from falling, sinking, or slipping; To be able to bear—withstand; To keep from falling or yielding during stress; To furnish corroborating evidence; To aid the cause of by approving, favoring, or advocating; To take action." What a wonderful definition! Believe me, every single word applies to the experience of belonging to a cancer patient support group.

There was a time when I couldn't even imagine attending a support group. Who wants to sit around with a bunch of depressed cancer patients, each with his or her sad story? How wrong I was! The people who attend support groups are the people who refuse to sit home and be sad and depressed. They choose to be active and take charge—to help themselves, as well as others. Obviously I had not yet looked up the word support!

Yes, cancers are different, and every case is unique and distinct. But the feelings, concerns, and fears that we have are all very much alike. Whatever you are feeling, one hour with a cancer support group will convince you that you are not alone in it.

※

This statement is so true: "A single arrow can be easily snapped in two, but a tight little bundle of arrows can withstand the strongest pressures."

※

Support groups give you overwhelming validation that others have felt the way you now feel and survived.

※

When we come together in a cancer support group we speak to each other much as I would imagine war veterans do—not as soldier to politician, or soldier to civilian—but soldier to soldier, for we have all shared the same trenches.

※

Think of a visit to your support group as a trip to the doctor for your mind and heart. You'll receive medicine, salve and soothing balms in the form of understanding, knowledge, shared experience, success stories, and personal empowerment. If it were written on a pre-scription pad it might read, "Take as needed, refill often, and if necessary call any one of us at any time." Now that is a prescription we all can use!

🌿

Even God thought support groups were important—that's why He made families.

🌿

When we reach out to someone, it is like throwing a pebble in a pool of water. You never know where the ripples will end.

🌿

Make your space your own: If you need to go into the hospital, take something familiar and comforting—the grown-up version of "night-night bear", maybe a comfy afghan that you like. Make your space your own; even if you are just there for an infusion, it can make a big difference. Curl up in the chair and take your shoes off. Don't be afraid of inconveniencing anyone by making yourself at home. Believe me, you are paying more for that little recliner chair than you ever did for any hotel room—so do your best to be comfortable.

❦

For an extended stay: If you must go into the hospital for an extended stay, even just for a few days, take a bedside light. When I went in for bone marrow, I did more than that. If I had to give up my entire house for 31 days, I would have to make my hospital room more "me." So I took a big puffy comforter (a twin size fits perfectly). I took silk plants, a small snap-together set of bookshelves and family pictures. But I think the thing I liked best was a little round lamp that I got at Kmart for $10. It had a dark green shade so it gave off a soft, subtle light. In the evening it softened the edges and made my room more homey and cozy. Even the nurses began to turn it on instead of the harsh overhead lights

when they came in. You'll be surprised at the difference
it makes.

My comforter was mostly white with big mauve peonies
and dark forest green leaves. I happened to be in a
room that had mauve curtains and pullbacks and green
chairs. I moved the other nightstand between the two
chairs and had a plant on it. It really was quite cozy.
One morning one of my doctors was seen going into my
room with some paperwork. The nurse stopped him
and said that I was down having a test. He said that he
knew, but that my room was the most comfortable and
inviting place to sit and do my chart. We all had a good
laugh. Personalizing my room really did make a difference; it affected attitudes, both mine and the staff's.

✤

Privacy: Cancer is peppered with losses, not the least
of which is privacy, particularly in the hospital. We are
poked, prodded, measured, weighed, examined, and
exposed. Take back control where and when you can. It
has always been important to me to shut the door to
my room whenever possible. Just having someone tap
before entering gives you back some dignity.

✤

Wear your own clothes. Nothing strips you of your
identity more then hospital garb. I remember reading

the story of a famous surgeon who became a patient.
He was amazed at how it felt to be on the other side of
the bed. The minute they took his clothes he felt as if
he lost some credibility and self-confidence. I know the
feeling. Even when visiting a trusted doctor, it's difficult
to feel on equal footing when you're wearing a paper
gown and socks and your feet don't touch the floor. So,
whenever possible ask if you can get dressed and then
talk. It really does make a difference. We feel less
vulnerable, more in control, better prepared.

🌿

Curl up with a loved one. When I was a little girl and
was in the hospital, there were all kinds of rules about
visiting hours and even about sitting on the bed. Thank-
fully that has changed. Nothing can break down the
barriers more than having a spouse lie with you once in
a while. On some nights, my husband and I curled up
side by side and watched television; it was so much
more "normal" than him in the chair and me in the bed.

🌿

Touching encouraged! Never minimize the importance of touch, especially in the hospital. The husband of
a dear friend of mine called me one night. "Darlin'," he
said, "Momma is having a real hard time, can you come?"

I went, she was in no immediate danger, but it seemed that there had been one complication after another, and her loving hubby could read her so well. She was momentarily depressed and completely done in.

I laid my head on her pillow and put a hand on her face and brow; we talked of how rough it had been for her, of what she had come through. She asked if I had ever felt as she was feeling, and I assured her I had—that it was possible to feel that bad and still feel good again. Sure enough, a couple days later Marie was feeling much better. She recalled how I had laid my head on her pillow, how she didn't have to look up at me, how she suddenly felt less removed. That was exactly what she had needed that night, and she asked how I had known. "I've been there, too," I said, and we both smiled as a thousand unspoken words passed between us.

✤

Visitors welcome: It's funny how cancer changes things, our image of ourselves and the image others have of us. How separate we often try to keep the healthy us and the sick us. How vulnerable the apparatus of cancer makes us. I had seen my friend, Dawn, all along during my treatment. She cut my hair for me in preparation for losing it; she pledged her bridal dance to raise funds for my transplant; she knew up close what was going on.

But it wasn't until she surprised me with a visit to the hospital during my transplant that we really had to face the reality of the disease together. I saw everything so clearly in her eyes, my vulnerability, her fear and sorrow, our disbelief. We didn't talk about any of it that day, but I know that it shook us both—the nakedness of illness, the in-your-face reality of it all. We were different, now, and these circumstances had changed us, that is true. But we weren't anything less, we were more.

*

Leaving the hospital: I remember vividly the day I first stepped outside after bone marrow treatment. Oh, if that wonderful rush of the senses could be bottled, it would be worth a thousand times its weight in gold!

It was a beautiful summer day, but beautiful is inadequate. The colors that day were turned up, as if I had been seeing with poor reception before. The scents in the air were almost overpowering. I could smell fresh-cut grass, growing flowers, traffic, food—I could *smell* the time of day. Morning smells different than evening or mid-day.

The sounds rushed at me. Voices, no longer filtered or contained by hospital walls, had a different ring outside. I heard a dog bark, a horn honk, a child yell, shoes hitting pavement, and multiple conversations going on around me. And the *feeling*—there was a slight breeze and I could feel my skin. It was almost as if the air itself had texture as it touched my face and arms. The sun, it warmed me from the outside in. Even walking felt different than it had in hospital corridors.

Had the world always been like this, this *alive*? I vowed to always look at life this way, to never forget this moment. Well, I'm afraid such delicious intensity can't last, but I do remember—oh, do I remember what it was like to be reborn.

🌾

Let's start with Death. There, I said the "D" word.

❦

There aren't many boogey men left in adult life, things that really scare us (besides the Nasdaq, of course) but cancer is one that does remain. When someone receives a diagnosis of cancer, the thought of death will inevitably rear its head. This is normal and natural. That said, cancer is not an automatic death sentence. Many more people survive cancer than die of it.

❦

Yes, people die of cancer, but the only people who can be assured of death from cancer are those who choose not to fight.

❦

True story: Cancer Treatment Centers of America holds a celebration every year. They invite back all the patients who have reached their five-year cancer-free mark and each person plants a tree. CTCA's goal is to plant a forest of cancer survivors. It is a *wonderful* celebration. One year Roger Cary, the CEO of CTCA, asked if any of the survivors had anything they wanted to say and a woman stood up. She recalled that one day, five years earlier, she had been sitting in her living room with a gun in her hand. That day, she had decided that she wasn't going to wait for cancer to kill her—that she would take matters into her own hands. The television was on and a commercial for Cancer Treatment Centers of America popped up on the screen. The word "cancer" grabbed her attention. The woman in the commercial, a former patient, said that cancer need not be a death sentence. Immediately, the other woman put the gun down, washed her face, and called the number. That day she planted her tree.

※

I have seen people who have chosen death over treatment. How sad. As a poet once wrote, "The saddest words of tongue or pen are these four words—what might have been." Go ahead and hold death as your trump card, if you must. After all, you can play that card anytime you wish—but I'm here to tell you that it's not the only card you hold.

※

A man once told me that he was thinking of suicide; he nobly wanted to save his family the ordeal of a cancer battle. If you are contemplating anything that drastic, let's at least be honest. Suicide does not save your family from anything. If you are doing it for your family's sake, which would they actually prefer: If you must go, would they prefer that you go out fighting, or would they rather have you leave them with the hardest thoughts of all—"would've, should've, could've?"

🌿

At the moment of our birth, God gave each of us a song to sing. It is we who must remember that it is not how long the song, but that we sing at all.

🌿

We will all die someday, that is a given, but let us each die but once—not each day by letting cancer, or anything else, steal the goodness from our days.

🌿

If we must die, let it be from the cancer and not from any statistics. Case in point—ME. Statistically, I should be long dead and buried, but I'm alive and kicking, thank you very much.

🌿

Fear can be a great motivator, a call to action, or it can be paralyzing. Don't let fear make you a deer in the headlights. Many deer end up dead, not because there wasn't safety nearby, but because they were too afraid to move.

🌿

LIFE AND DEATH

We can always play our trump card—we can always choose later to stop treatment, but only if we first choose to start.

＊

You say your odds aren't very good? Look at MY odds! Odds never stopped us from cheering for a hometown football team. It is even sweeter when the underdog wins. Give yourself a chance to suit up, play and win.

＊

Mara, my wonderful Mara, gave me a 3-by-8 card that provided the insight and courage I needed to begin my treatment. When Doctor M first saw all my scans and slides he recommended twelve months of intense chemotherapy. *Twelve months!* It was intimidating. Then Mara gave me that little card:

> *Today I believe I can win, today I choose to fight.*
> *But I reserve the right to quit tomorrow without*
> *feeling guilty or like I have let anyone down.*

Looking back, I think that statement would have been even more powerful and real if it had been worded this way: "Today I think *maybe* I can win." Or even, "Today I doubt it, but there is a slight *possibility* that I can win, so today I choose to fight."

＊

Yes, yes, I can hear you saying, "Vickie, this is all well and good but what about the 'what ifs' that I feel? I've chosen to fight and will do so, but sometimes, sometimes…"

Believe me, I understand. We all experience the dreaded "what ifs." The question is how do we handle them? If we express our doubts to our loved ones, we hear a horrified, "Don't think that way!" But denying that we occasionally have thoughts of death is again like ignoring that big pink elephant in the middle of the living room.

So what do we do? If we can't get rid of the elephant entirely, I say let's at least make it dance for us. By this I mean that we do everything in our power to affect the outcome, to make it a positive one. We choose our doctors and hospitals very carefully. I believe very strongly that we add a good nutritionist and naturopath to our team of doctors. We take care of ourselves, eat what we should, take our vitamins and supplements religiously. We exercise, drink water, use relaxation. We top it off with the best mental and spiritual support we can find. We make our peace with friends, family, and our God. If it makes you feel better, make out your will. When you have done all that you possibly can, then even the "what ifs" are taken care of.

🌿

When we open ourselves to sharing our cancer journeys with each other, so too do we open ourselves to the possible pain of losing someone who has become a part of who we are. But I would not change one moment of the time I have shared with all the wonderful, remarkable, amazing people I've met—even knowing the huge hole some have left in my life with their passing.

☙

Death takes many forms. There is young death, old death, surprise death, and death due to illness. Trying to shield ourselves from death would be to never again hold a newborn baby, for death is as natural as birth.

☙

Cancer plays no favorites. I was once wandering the halls of CTCA and saw a woman sitting alone, the now-familiar look of concern so evident on her face. I stopped to talk, as I often do in such circumstances. She said her name was Connie, and it was her husband she was worried about. She expressed the same sadness and fears that all our loved ones face. Her husband was the legendary Walter Payton, the one-and-only "Sweetness," formerly Number 34 for the Chicago Bears.

It was a thrill for me to meet the football hero whose

abilities I had so loved to watch, but it was an *honor* for me to meet Walter, the man. We talked of the horrors of this disease. His difficulties were the same as yours and mine, except more public. The stickers in the CAT scan even earned me one of those million-dollar smiles.

Yes, this disease has stolen many wonderful people from us. I was in Chicago when Walter Payton died. I witnessed an entire city come to a standstill and cry as the nation mourned with them. Walter Payton was a hero, both on and off the field, and his wonderful wife Connie and the Payton family have continued the charitable works so important to Walter by establishing the Walter Payton Cancer Fund.

Walter is gone, but his legacy and good works live on. Walter didn't lose; no one loses their battle to cancer. In order for the cancer to win, it would have to be able to follow us beyond the grave. It cannot do so. When our bodies give out, so too does the cancer. And Heaven is certainly not a consolation prize for having lost something.

☙

Sometimes I think God just looks down and says, "Enough—come home."

☙

On the most difficult day of my life, Father Leo eased
the pain somewhat with a metaphor. He said that life
was like a day in the park. Some kids get to stay and
play all day, some until mid-day, and some just get to play
for the morning. Then their Father comes to call them
home. It is we who are left who must remember that
home is not a bad place to be.

It made me think of my own family. There were five kids
and we all loved to play outside. We would play and play
until my mom or dad would finally make us come inside.
We always whined about coming in, and we always
postponed it as long as we could. But, once inside, we
all knew that our home was a wonderful place. Mom
and Dad really did know best; I have to think that God
does, too.

❦

I've always hated new shoes. They hurt my feet until
they are broken in. I think life is much like that. Life
doesn't get comfortable until middle age or so. But even
I must admit that there comes a time when the best of
old shoes become too worn, when they pinch the feet
or get a hole, when they can no longer be mended.
Then, no matter how much we've loved those shoes, it
is time to get a new pair. Now, that doesn't mean that

we stop walking, it just means we've traded one pair of shoes for another. I like to think of life and death that way.

✤

End-stage cancer can become like a full-body cast, holding back the vibrant, vivacious, outgoing person inside. To shed this cast so that we can once again soar is not a bad thing.

✤

The only thing that cancer ever claims is a tired, worn body and even that is a hollow victory, for it can never claim our soul.

✤

I believe that God gives terminal cancer patients a gift that most others never get. We know when our time is drawing near. It is like receiving an invitation for a vacation in advance and having an opportunity to get ready. We can pack our gear, take care of things left undone, say our good-byes and prepare for the journey. Like any other journey, please let us talk about it with you if we want. Don't waste time denying that we are going, for when it is time, we will leave.

✤

LIFE AND DEATH

When we love someone, we often want to keep him or her with us at all cost. I, too, have been guilty of this. I once realized, to my horror, that I was holding earth-bound a dear friend of mine. She was like a free spirit, like a kite or a balloon on a string; she was pulling at her tether, which was her love and loyalty to those of us still with feet of clay. With the greatest gift of love we could bestow, we finally cut the tether and set her free. Her body left us, but her spirit never will.

❧

I know it is extremely difficult for our doctors and care providers when they are unable to save us all. My dear friend, Frankie, and I once tried to ease this pain some-what. I had gone to spend what I knew to be some final hours with Frankie. We talked of so many things, we laughed, we cried, and we shared what was most impor-tant with each other. There wasn't time for trivial things. One concern that Frankie entrusted to my care was to try to ease the pain of her passing for all those who loved her at Cancer Treatment Centers of America. Ultimately, they had been unable to save her, but they had picked her up, as they had me, at the end of the line and given her three and a half more years of life— quality life filled with love, family and friends, not just time.

LIFE AND DEATH

Frankie wanted the CTCA staff to know how much she appreciated what they had done for her—and to let them know that it was okay. Finally I said, "Okay, Frankie, on the day you leave us I will send a big bouquet of balloons to them, along with a note from you telling them that you are free." My dear friend smiled at me and said that was perfect. A few minutes later, however, she said in her bare whisper, "Vic, better idea. Send one balloon a day for 30 days. Jim will pay you." That was my Frankie. I told her not to worry, that I would take care of it for her.

On the day Frankie passed on (not away), the first balloon was delivered by a wonderful lady named Donna. When I had explained to her what I wanted to do, she had refused to accept any money. People are truly amazing; she said that she would personally send a different balloon each day for a month. The first one was a big smiley face with those crinkly arms and legs. I had her attach a note from Frankie telling all the CTCA staff that she loved them and was now free; she was home and would now watch over them. I later talked to the staff, and I learned that the balloons had made an amazing difference to them. They hadn't let Frankie down, and Frankie knew it.

🌾

I have a theory on life, that it is much like music. I believe that a well-lived life plays on forever in the minds, the hearts, and in the very souls of all who hear it. That each life's song is but a blend of the notes given to us by God at the moment of our birth. We put the story to the melodies that we choose by the way we live each day. Throughout our lives, we add to this mix the notes from the lives of all who touch us deeply. And they, in turn, live on in us—and the music continues.

🌿

Even a grounded bird can sing, and sometimes its song is the most beautiful song of all.

🌿

FAITH AND PRAYER

Never forget that you have a toll-free, never-busy, direct line from your heart to God's ear.

🌿

As my mom says, "God never takes His phone off the hook."

🌿

When I was a little girl I was admitted to the hospital quite a few times for heart problems. I always felt safer when my mom or dad was there. No matter what happened to me, it was easier to endure when they were in the hospital, even if they had to step out into the hall and were out of sight. I had total faith that they would not leave my door and would be right there if I really needed them. How wonderful if we could summon the same faith in God. He is, after all, just outside the door.

🌿

No faith? Ask for some! It's perfectly okay to ask God to increase your faith. And remember, too, that He has given us teachers here on earth. Don't be afraid to reach out to a Chaplain, Minister, Priest, or Rabbi. Whatever is

FAITH AND PRAYER

bothering you, be specific and direct about your questions—they can take it. That's why their Boss called them to the job.

🌿

While you're at it, remember that your "soul keeper" of choice is a wonderful person to discuss the issue of death and dying with. This is the one person who is not going to say, "Oh, don't talk that way." Your chaplain or minister will not break down, and you don't have to be careful about his or her feelings. Remember, they love you and want to help—that is why they chose to do what they do.

🌿

God works through others—so pay attention.

🌿

The best way to realize how much faith you have is to offer to help someone else find or renew theirs.

🌿

The amazing thing about prayer is that it equally helps the pray-er and the pray-ee.

🌿

Maybe if we were charged a fee to pray we would have a better sense of its value. Of course, no one could afford it, for the value of prayer is priceless.

🌿

God expects us to do what we can to help ourselves. A pastor friend of mine says, "In a storm you should pray to high heaven, but continue to row the boat to shore."

🌿

I once met a man who was trying to avoid treatment for his cancer. He told me that if God wanted him healed, He could do so without surgery or chemo. "True," I said to him, "and with that theory you can skip dinner because if God wants food in your tummy, He can certainly put it there." End of argument.

🌿

God has given us all a spirit that will soar, if we only give it half a chance.

🌿

I believe that God sent us to earth with everything that we would ever need to survive. Think about it. He sent Adam and Eve to earth with fingerprints. Why—so they could identify each other? No, because He knew that someday fingerprints would be important to society. The one thing He didn't feel would ever be important is an expiration date. Think how simple it would have been. God could have stamped the bottom of one of our feet with a date, but He chose not to. I believe it's because He knows us so well. Think of all the love lost and the beauty missed for tears too early shed. If God gave you no expiration date, let no one else give you one!

※

A wonderful woman led the children's choir when I was a child (when you're little, they let anyone sing, even me). She once said that if you have trouble praying, just ask God to come and sit on your bed or to pull up a chair. Then talk to Him as you would a friend. I think that's pretty good advice for grown-ups, too.

※

A desperate woman wanted to know how I had asked God to heal me, as if I had used some magic words. My heart broke. I told her that I was sure I had asked in much the same way that she was asking. I'm certain that prayers are not answered based on the beauty or eloquence of the words. After all, would any earthly mother or father refuse to help one of their children, simply because they didn't ask properly? Of course not, and neither would your heavenly Father. But just as we can't always give our children everything they desire, He too knows what's best for us. Sometimes we just have to trust in an unspoken, "Because I said so," from Him, too.

❦

They say God will never fill your cup too full. Well, I'm sure that's true, but I also think His cups must come with saucers, and sometimes He doesn't count what splashes over.

❦

Having faith doesn't mean that we never wonder why we got cancer, only that we believe that God has an answer for all that we go through. During the worst part of her battle with cancer, one of my dearest friends, a woman of limitless faith, said it best: "God sure has a lot of explaining to do when I get there."

❦

It's okay to be mad at God sometimes, just don't refuse to talk to Him about it.

❦

FAITH AND PRAYER

Sometimes it may feel as if God has turned His back on us—but it's actually the other way around. Our backs may have been turned toward God—for He has never turned His back to us.

❦

Try to look at the "silences" from God as His way of giving us time to work things out for ourselves. When we are helping our children with their homework, we don't just give them the answers. Instead we provide them with the tools they need to figure it out for themselves. So keep your eyes and ears open for the "tools" that God is giving you.

❦

Tears: If God hadn't meant for us to cry, He wouldn't have given us tear ducts. Tears are God's way of cleansing and washing away. Sometimes tears wash away a speck of dirt in our eye, and sometimes they wash away a bit of something in our hearts or minds.

❦

I remember stoically hanging on for so long, through all the early diagnoses and rejections. Then I found Cancer Treatment Centers and they finally gave me hope and I just fell apart. I cried and cried. Those tears helped clean the slate so I could start fresh. Thank you, God.

❦

FAITH AND PRAYER

I love and took comfort from the passage that God knows and cares when a sparrow falls from a tree. If He knows the pain of a sparrow, He certainly knows ours. Just realizing that He understands makes it easier.

🌿

God only made each day to be 24 hours long because He knew that's about all we can handle. When we get into trouble, it is often because we are either hanging on to hours from yesterday, or borrowing them from tomorrow.

🌿

By the way, cancer is not a punishment for anything that you have or have not done! That is not how it works. Hitler didn't have cancer, and neither did Attila the Hun. I could go on and on, but I'm sure you get the point.

🌿

Many years ago my fiancé, Bart, was killed instantly in a car accident. I've never been more devastated; afterwards I didn't think life was worth living. For a long time afterwards I was just putting in time. During this period, Bart's wonderful mom sent me a saying: "Our life comes to an end when God comes to the end of our rope, not when we do." Little did she know how often I would turn to that slip of paper I carried in my purse.

I learned way back then that sometimes the best we can

do when we get to the end of our rope is to just tie a knot and hang on. I would never have believed then that I would someday fight for my life. But He knew, and He also knew that cancer would only be the second hardest battle I had ever fought.

🌿

Because of my faith I was never really afraid of being dead, it was the getting there that gave me qualms.

🌿

I thank God that my life didn't come with previews. I might have thought it was too frightening to stay for the feature presentation and missed some really great parts.

🌿

If we just had a crystal ball and could gaze into the future and see that the outcome was going to be fine, it would certainly make the treatment easier. Wait a minute, we do. If we trust in God, the outcome will be fine.

🌿

Billy Graham once said, "I try not to worry about life too much because I read the last page of *the* book and it all turns out all right." I like that.

🌿

TREATMENT'S OVER

I've described coming to the end of your cancer treatment as somewhat like a dog chasing a car and actually catching it. Now what do you do?

❦

For weeks or months we yearn for the end of treatment. We *pray* for the end of treatment. Suddenly it's over and, at first, we rejoice, "Yeah, yeah, yeah, no more treatment!" Then reality sets in and our mind starts second-guessing:

- Are they *sure* I don't need any more treatment?
- I needed treatment this month, how do they know I won't need it next month?
- Did they really get it all?
- If they don't know what caused it in the beginning, how can I be sure that it won't come back?
- Are they sure about removing the port? Maybe we should leave it in just a little while longer.
- Jeez, three more months before next testing—is that too long? What if it comes back right away?

These are normal concerns. In general, the longer you are on treatment, and the better you respond, the harder it is to psychologically let go. Also, the sicker you were when you began, the harder it is to stop. The mind says, "Look how sick I was before I started treatment—what if I go back to that?"

My suggestion is to simply remind yourself that you have done all that was asked of you and more. Every athlete, entertainer, or musician wonders if they have practiced enough as they are about to step out on the field or stage—but they go right ahead and step out there anyway. The same is true for us. There comes a time when every cancer survivor must simply step out the door and do it—and for us, the "it" is to live.

❦

I would have never guessed it possible, but when the doctors finally came to remove my chemo port, I asked them if they were sure. When the first 21 days rolled by and for the first time in over a year I wasn't returning for treatment, it was a mixed blessing. Of course I was elated to be off chemotherapy (I'm not totally crazy), but I was concerned. I had come so far—I didn't want to slip back. Who would be monitoring me now—just *me*?

❦

I think that our mother's apron strings are probably easier to cut than the chemotherapy line—for chemo has literally been our lifeline. This is particularly true if you have been left with nothing more after treatment than to *hope* it doesn't return.

🌾

I believe with all my heart that we must do more than *hope* that our cancer doesn't return. I take comfort from the fact that my treatment plan cares for me in my wellness as well as in my illness. I have stayed with the nutritional program that helped me regain my health. Will everyone who eats right and takes supplements be able to avoid a reoccurrence? No, but I do know that a well-nourished person is better able to retain and, when need be, regain their health.

🌾

One physician said to me, "If it ain't broke, don't fix it." Well, I'll agree with that and go one further: "If it was broke, make *sure* you've fixed it."

When your treatment is over, stack the deck in your favor—do whatever it takes to maintain a healthy immune system. I believe my continuing success and safety come from having altered a path twice traveled and arriving at a different location this time. They say the proof is in the pudding. Well, this little pudding is still doing A-OK.

🌾

TREATMENT'S OVER

Some people assume that just because they are no longer receiving treatments they must be "back to normal." Not true on two counts: First, the body itself has to recover from what it's been through, but not just the body, the mind and the heart must also recover. Let's face it—this is not like recovering from the flu or the chicken pox. A cancer diagnosis shakes you right to the core. We lose whatever naiveté we once had that this couldn't happen to us. You may be able to let go of your oncologist before you let go of your counselor or therapist. The mind and the body do not always heal at the same pace—but heal they do.

☙

Often too, we are left with physical changes that have occurred. Well, of course you are happy that you're alive and, yes, it was worth the sacrifice—but that doesn't make it easy to lose a breast, or a prostate, or a colon, or a lung, or a kidney. Feel free to mourn for a while, but if you can't shake it, talk to someone. Attend support groups that share your concerns. Make yourself look at your situation through a loved one's eyes. If your spouse or friend had had a mastectomy, would you still love them? Of course you would. Well then, give them as much credit for being the same caliber spouse or friend.

☙

Sometimes we must realize that it is only we who have the problem with our new selves, and we must attack this problem with the same energy we brought to the cancer. For, no matter what we've lost, we are always much more than the sum total of our parts. In a fight against cancer I now realize that you always gain far more than you lose. It's just going to take some adjusting—this too you can do.

꧁

My mom after her mastectomy: "Maybe my golf swing will improve." What an attitude! Does that mean it didn't bother her? Of course not, but she chose to look at the positive side. I am so grateful for her courage and smarts. She lost a breast, but my God, we could have lost her, and she us—that puts it all in perspective.

꧁

Remember we had aches and pains before cancer, just as we do now. Every one of your aches and pains is *not* cancer.

It sometimes happens. Cancer, once beaten, can return. Former British Prime Minister Margaret Thatcher said it best: "You may have to fight a battle more than once to win it."

❦

I once got a card that showed a teddy bear sitting on the floor with some of its cotton hanging out. It said, "Ever feel as if you've had the stuffin' knocked out of you?" I loved that card. A reoccurrence of cancer feels like that. But remember, our most-loved toys were often mended more than once.

❦

Re-diagnosis is completely different from a first diagnosis. Everyone feels as if, "Here we go again"— that they somehow *failed*. Not true! You knocked it out once. There is no reason to think that you can't knock it out again.

❦

Yes, but what if the second diagnosis is worse than the first? In certain ways, cancer is cancer, folks. I've had some Stage One and Stage Two patients tell me that they are not so sure that they would be able to deal with Stage Three or Stage Four. Trust me, if you've dealt with cancer at any stage, you have all the tools you need. It's just that you don't *know* it beforehand.

≈

I look at re-diagnosis as two fighters in the ring. At the sound of the first bell, neither can knock the other out. But with each treatment (round), the cancer recuperates less and less, giving you a better chance to finally knock it senseless. A re-diagnosis just means that cancer got up off the mat for one more round. Remember it was the cancer that wore out the first time—not you.

≈

This time you *know* your hair will come back.

≈

Of course, the best way to avoid reoccurrence is to do everything in your power to prevent it. Think of it this way: If you follow the same set of directions to any given location, chances are you will reach it. That's how we get to the same mall, again and again. If you want to arrive at a different destination, you must change the directions. The second time around I changed some of the directions in my life and thus far have avoided a path twice traveled. Dang it all, dark leafy greens really *are* better for you than chocolate cake.

≈

RE-DIAGNOSIS

How do you ever feel totally safe again? It's difficult. In my case I was told that I could *never* get cancer free, and then they hedged their bets by saying that even if I did, it would definitely reoccur. Jeez, the power of positive thinking—how do I deal with *that*?

Well, I've dealt with it by choosing to live my life somewhat like a picnic on a cloudy day. I've gone ahead and planned the picnic, made the food, packed the car, gone to a great location, and am having a blast—even though the weatherman still says there's a chance of showers.

I have two choices: I can either let the prediction of rain ruin everything as much as the rain itself would (and this still wouldn't prevent the rain from falling if it is going to). Or I can throw some rain gear in the car just in case—in the trunk, out of sight—and enjoy every minute of sunshine that I have. It may not rain at all or, if it does, it may just sprinkle—but I've made up my mind that the mere "possibility" of rain will not rob me of even one second before it falls.

So far, I have enjoyed seven consecutive storm-free years. Enjoy the sunshine. If the rain falls, I'll deal with it then, but I have had some wonderful picnics in the meantime.

Even if your battle with cancer is ongoing, please don't bypass the "Survivor" or "Success Stories" sections in this book. Actually these two chapters may be even more important *during* your struggles than after. The moment you survive the diagnosis you become a survivor, and the moment your cancer has been detected your success story begins. So please read on.

✻

Everything and anything is easier if not done alone. You are not alone! This entire nation, including your own city, community and neighborhood, is populated with survivors—everyday people who have beaten, and are beating, this disease. Let the knowledge of their success fuel yours.

✻

True, not everyone with cancer recovers, but far more do than don't. I wish there were magic glasses that you could wear while walking in the mall or at a sporting event—glasses that would clearly show you all the cancer survivors in the crowd. You would be absolutely amazed at how many you would see. And each of them at some point felt as you have felt, or may be feeling now.

🌾

When survivors meet, a momentary flicker passes between the eyes, as if to say, "I know, I've been there, and I too have come out the other side."

🌾

Whether your cancer is blessedly in remission or whether your battle rages on, each and every day we are all survivors.

🌾

Every day after diagnosis that we continue to live and breathe and love—we are survivors.

🌾

Today you got up; therefore you are a survivor. If you are reading this in bed, then today you woke up and that makes you a survivor.

🌾

Wear your survivorship as a badge of honor for all to see so they won't be so afraid to fight the bully.

🌾

Share your success with the children. Let them grow up knowing that cancer is not always the end of the road, it is usually just a bend in the road.

🌿

Take your children, your grandchildren, your nieces and nephews with you to the cancer walks, the marches, and the runs. Let them learn and see what true courage is. Help them understand the importance of getting involved. Let them learn early not to sit back and complain, but to move forward and to support change.

🌿

When we teach children that the bully can be beaten, they, in turn, will not be so afraid to fight, if fight they must.

🌿

Many people, even after recovering from cancer, find that they have somehow lost faith in their bodies. They feel that their body is not as good as before. Your body is not damaged goods! As a matter of fact, your body is an Olympic champion. It met and defeated the enemy. If anything your body is better; you have been through the test of fire and were victorious. Wear your medal proudly.

🌿

ON BEING A SURVIVOR

After we are well, I think it is even more important that we continue to attend marches, rallies, runs, and support groups. Two reasons: first, our success is the best medicine for those who continue to struggle; second, we now have the strength to help carry the torch for those who may momentarily find it too heavy to carry alone.

People who have never had cancer can champion the cause and talk of what "could be." People who currently have cancer can champion the cause and talk of what "should be." People who have prevailed can champion the cause and tell of what "must be."

It is said that old soldiers never die nor ever tire of reliving the glories of their battles, of the loyalties of their comrades, both the fallen and the survivors. As soldiers in the battle against cancer, we can now better understand. For, if we live to be a hundred, this is a battle that we will always be proud to have fought and to have shared with those who fought with us—those both living and fallen. For we have learned, as every soldier does, that it is not necessarily the outcome that matters—it is having risen to the fight that counts.

Let's spread our survivorship around. It is amazing what we tried-and-true champion fighters can accomplish when we set our minds to it. At Cancer Treatment Centers of America, for example, we the patients and former patients decided that we wanted to spread the word about the importance of the "patient empowerment" treatment we had found. Because CTCA patients come from all over the world it was difficult to form the usual support group, so we went to CTCA and asked for help. If we could assemble groups of neighbors, friends, church members, etc. in our own communities, would CTCA be willing to send someone to speak about the success of empowered patient care, of nutrition, of spirituality? Yes, they would—and that's how the *Cancer Fighter Program* began.

I feel very proud and passionate about this program. *Cancer Fighters* are dedicated to making a difference in the lives of cancer patients everywhere. We now travel all across the country sharing vital knowledge, hope and inspiration wherever groups of 200-plus are gathered. If you would like to jump onboard with us, we'd love to have you. Look for contact information in the Resource Section at the back of the book.

❦

ON BEING A SURVIVOR

People have told me that I have been to hell and back, and once I might have agreed. But now, with a little more distance, I know better. For this journey that I took so reluctantly has opened my eyes to scenery, the beauty of which I might otherwise have missed.
When I think of all the people who fought for me and with me, those who have crossed my path only because of cancer, I now realize that, yes God took me to the brink of something. But I now believe it was heaven I caught a glimpse of, and I will be forever grateful for the view.

✺

SUCCESS STORIES

A success story is like finding another American in a foreign country.

❦

Success stories are food for our hearts and souls. Success stories should be shouted from the highest rooftops: "I beat it! I beat it! I beat it! I beat it!"

❦

When I was a little girl I had terrible nightmares. I would cry out and my mom would come into my room and turn on the light. The monsters of my dreams couldn't stand up to her presence or to the light. The monster sitting on the end of the bed again became a pile of clothes. The one on the other side of the room again became the closet door. That is what happens to cancer when we throw the brilliant light of a success story on it. Use others' successes to light up the darkest recesses of your mind and heart—the places where the monsters most often lurk.

❦

By sharing success stories, you help destroy the monster, slay the dragon, and send the bully called cancer running for all of us. It is not enough just to defeat cancer. No, we must tell others and share our victories so that others in turn will not be so afraid to fight.

❧

Success stories save lives.

❧

Oh, but I hear you saying, "I still have such a long way to go." Remember that each cancer success story—and there are countless thousands of them—began with a first step.

❧

Celebrate your conquests, both large and small. Within one cancer battle there are many individual success stories—first steps taken, fears faced and conquered, tears shed and dried. Starting today, celebrate them all!

❧

Success is sometimes just getting out of bed.

❧

Success is sometimes staying in bed.

❧

Success is surviving; you are surviving; you are a success.

❧

SURVIVOR'S GUILT

Survivors' guilt—I too have dealt with this. Why do some get well and others don't? Why did I get well? I remember reading about survivor's guilt when I was fighting, and I thought, "Ah, sure, let me get well and I'll deal with the guilt." It is not always so easy.

✺

One woman once asked me somewhat bitterly what I had done differently than her mom to survive. My answer was that I could not tell her what I had done differently, but I could tell her what I had not done. I had not fought any harder, or been any braver or stronger than her mom. I hadn't wanted to live any more nor die any less. Of that I could assure her.

✺

One young girl gave me the most wonderful gift. As I held her in my arms at her own mother's funeral and tried to comfort her, my own tears began to fall. She looked up at me and understood what I would never have tried to explain. She said, "Oh, Vickie, it's okay to cry because my mom is gone, but never cry because you survived. It wasn't an either/or proposition." Out of the mouths of babes.

✺

SURVIVOR'S GUILT

Being a hero has nothing whatsoever to do with the outcome of a battle. Remember the Alamo.

✤

Not long ago I lost two very good friends, back to back. These two deaths sent me reeling. I tried all the things that I have done to recover from loss in the past. I told myself all the right things. I knew my pain was selfish pain, but still it hurt.

It seems that over these many years, I have had an endless series of cancer friends. First came the friends who fought with me, and then came the friends I worked with when I first got well, and then came the friends after that, and on it goes. It sometimes seems like I am Grand Central Station. I stay in place as so many pass in and out of my life. We spend time together during the chaotic interim until they are once again on a train. Some go on to good health and new adventures, and some are taking their final journey home.

But this time seemed too much. Losing these two friends so swiftly and so closely—this was more than even I could handle. This time I, too, thought about hopping the train and not looking back. Never again, I told myself! And for a few days I ran.

Then one night the phone rang and I heard a desperate voice saying that she had just been diagnosed and I found myself back on the tracks—dusting off train schedules, ticket prices, connecting routes, and all the rest. As I hung up the phone that night I swear I heard a distant laugh, a familiar voice echoing through the station. It was Frankie, just as sure as if she were still here with us—with Marie's chuckle in the background! I distinctly heard Frankie say, "We knew it, kid, you can't stop, we are all meant to do what we are meant to do—and for you, this is it."

So, yes, the trains still come and go and, God willing, I'll stay put awhile and complete my job. Yes, sometimes the farewells are sad, but while they are at the station, what a time we've had!

※

Survivor's guilt? There should be no such thing. Instead there should be survivor's anger. We're mad as hell that we all don't make it . . . yet!

※

INSURANCE
Shouting secrets in this section!!
(Just thought you should know)

The trials and tribulations of dealing with our insurance companies are a reality for every cancer patient. Insurance issues and problems brought me to my knees at least as often as the disease. Just know that, as in all other things, the first response from your insurance company is not necessarily the definitive one. I hope some of the following anecdotes will help.

※

I once gave a speech in which I detailed some of the horrific treatment I had endured at the hands of my insurance company. After the speech a high-ranking official from another major insurance company came up to me with tears in her eyes. She wouldn't give me her name, but she gave me two words—*case management*—and told me I was smart enough to figure out the rest. I did the legwork and soon discovered the "secret" she had been sharing with me, and I subsequently passed it along to countless others. Here it is: Think of case management as the process whereby your doctor or hospital invoices your insurance company for "individual itemized expenses" instead of one big procedure. I have seen the lion's share of $200,000 bone marrow transplants covered this way. Here's how it works:

Your insurance company may say that a bone marrow transplant is not covered by your policy, but you do have chemotherapy coverage, hospitalization coverage, CAT Scan coverage, etc. By breaking down the uncovered bone marrow transplant procedure into many component parts that are covered, your hospital may be able to help you get coverage for most of the Bone Marrow Transplant. The only items not covered in many cases are the harvest of the stem cells and the re-infusion. That changes things drastically from your being personally responsible for a $200,000 procedure to only being responsible for the $7,000–$15,000 harvest and re-infusion procedure. It doesn't always work, but I have seen it work many times.

When testifying before a Senate committee on health care, I used this example and told our fine Senators that women all across the country (for it is usually breast and ovarian claims that are turned down) were dying for less than the price of a new car and just didn't realize it. It at least momentarily got their attention. Now they know, and so do you.

✺

Another person in the insurance industry took me aside and shared this little gem about what to do if you are ever denied payment on a claim—especially if the treatment you received is considered to be an "iffy" or "questionable" procedure. He said there are certain procedures that are *automatically* denied by some insurance companies, basically because they know that three out of ten patients will meekly accept the denial without a fight. In essence, the insurance companies are "playing the odds" with your life.

For example, let's say ten people apply for coverage of a particular treatment procedure and all ten are automatically denied. The statistics show that only seven of the ten will ever reapply. Already, the insurance company saves the cost of those three procedures. When the other seven reapply, all are again denied. Statistics again show that, of those seven, only three will resubmit. The insurance company finally pays those three, but with just a little paper work they saved themselves the cost of covering the other seven procedures. I don't know why three is the magic number, but it seems to be—I've since seen it in operation.

✹

Just re-billing under a different code can cover many procedures for you. Again, encourage your doctor to be more creative—not dishonest, just more creative and persistent about helping you negotiate the pathetic maze of obstacles that insurance companies often throw in our path. Cancer support groups are valuable sources of information regarding insurance issues. It seems that every patient has an insurance "survival technique" to share.

✺

If at all possible *stay away from HMO's*—just my opinion, folks.

✺

Make some noise. It is much harder to do something rotten publicly than it is privately, even for an insurance company.

✺

When I received the denial for my bone marrow transplant I was devastated, then I got angry. I told a local newspaper that I had a story to tell and not a lot of time to tell it. It was a story that their readers needed to hear, a story that was being played out behind the closed doors of homes all across this country. They ran the story; other papers picked it up, and so did radio and television.

INSURANCE

Three weeks into this very public battle, I got a phone call from my insurance company telling me that my case had been "re-evaluated" and I now qualified for a transplant. I was ecstatic. Then the other shoe fell. They said there were two stipulations. One, I had to immediately cease and desist any publicity regarding my transplant. (Okay, I thought, this I can do; after all, I will be in the hospital for the next 30 days.) But the second was the kicker. I would have to sign a statement sealing the records and promising never to disclose that my transplant had been covered. This I could *not* do. Not only did I tell them no, but I included details of their little phone call in future interviews. How dare they!

✾

If you are having problems with your coverage, call and send a good old-fashioned personal letter to your congressmen, congresswomen, and senators. Tell them your story. I was very skeptical that this would do any good, but I was desperate. I got surprising results; they were interested. Eventually I spoke personally with Senators Don Reigle and Carl Levin. They put wonderful staff people on my case and made calls to the insurance company. This was very helpful; it convinced my insurance company that I was one client who was simply not going to go away.

✾

When you write your letter, attach a picture of yourself and your family. This is personal, this is your life—make it personal to your congressmen and senators, too. It is much harder to disregard someone you have seen— someone who is not just a social security number. Have your mother, father, siblings, friends, and neighbors write letters, too.

*

A Christmas story: While shopping for presents this year I saw Senator Reigle and his daughter pass in the crowd. Just seeing him made me smile. Then I thought, "I should let him know I made it, and share my success." So I tracked him down. I said that I didn't know if he would remember me or not but my name was Vickie and he had helped me live. He did remember, he hugged me and we both cried a little. I also took a minute to tell his young daughter what a great man her dad is— that I, and many others, are alive today because he cared.

*

We must make enough noise so that our legislative bodies can hear us—so that their vote can reflect our voice. We are already making a difference. Notice that virtually every politician now talks about health care reform. Believe me, there weren't many of them doing that in the early Nineties. They are talking now because we are demanding it—but the battle has just begun.

❦

Why be such a pain in the neck to your insurance company, why fight when they tell you "no"? Because this is life and death, folks...because you're a valuable and important human being (even though your insurance company may try to convince you otherwise)... because you deserve the most up-to-date treatment... and because I and all your friends and loved ones want you to get well.

❦

Phone calls like the one I received after a television interview really made the fight worthwhile: "Vickie, I called the station and got your number after seeing you. I have cancer too. I've been so sad, frightened, and overwhelmed since diagnosis and all the insurance problems that have followed; and I suddenly realized I've just been lying here waiting to die. After listening to you, I found your anger at the injustice contagious. Thank you for the bug—this is one I needed to catch."

❦

I agree that we need more research for bright new cancer-fighting procedures. My friends and I continue to march, walk and run for more research money. But my major cause over the last seven years has been to ensure that today's cancer patients have equal access to the very best treatment that is *already* available. For those who can't even access what is currently available, future breakthroughs are only a promise of more things they can't have!

❦

Go ahead and let your community and the public in general know how you feel. As things became increasingly clear to me, I took up a battle cry. I let everyone know that my insurance company wanted me to die quickly and silently and not cost them any more money. After all, I was supposed to be "terminal," right? I was supposed to die, right? So, why should they spend any more money on me, right? Wrong! I had no intention of dying, and I don't do anything silently. Like you, or anyone else for that matter, I deserved every available chance to get well—so they were in for a fight.

❦

INSURANCE

People have asked me how I got started speaking out. Well, it's true that necessity is the mother of invention. I spoke out because I had no choice. There were no conventional avenues left; they had all been closed to me. Sometimes this is a good thing; I think our best recipes have probably come when we run out of everything we normally use and have to improvise. I had tried everything except my own voice to state my own cause—the right to the treatment of my choice. When I went public, I learned that it wasn't my own cause—that the same insurance inequities were occurring behind closed doors all across the nation. This enraged me. I've not stopped speaking since.

✹

In the early days of my fight, a journalist urged me to openly describe what happens when someone receives a terminal diagnosis and an insurance denial in the Netherlands. She said, "If you're brave enough to tell the story, I'll do whatever it takes to get it printed. I was and she did. It was a powerful, eye-opening series of articles. Thank you, Joyce, for helping me open this travesty for public scrutiny. You were the first.

✹

I have found that it's actually easier to run with a banner in my hands—with a purpose—than it is to run empty-handed. The "cause" makes the running easier.

※

Whenever you see an article in the paper regarding an insurance issue, write in and add your two-cents' worth. Many of my friends wrote to the op-ed section of their papers. The more people who show a local interest in the insurance issue, the more response we will get on all fronts.

※

When friends and family ask if there is anything they can do, give them an assignment to contact someone for you. Believe me, they will be glad and feel helpful. We need the voices of the healthy to stand with us and for us if we are truly to make a difference.

※

Filing an insurance claim is difficult enough if you are well. But when you are tired and depleted from cancer treatment, every unnecessary phone call, bureaucratic holdup, or administrative obstacle can feel like a night-mare. I think many insurance companies realize they can wear us out. It reminds me of the childhood story of the tiger who ran around chasing his own tail until he turned into butter. They often try to run us around until we, too, have a meltdown—until we are too discouraged, too broke, or too sick to fight back. I've seen insurance companies knock the fight out of a person before the disease. This must stop!

🌿

The best outcome is for us to get well, and then continue to fight by adding our voice to others—not to frighten but to enlighten.

🌿

During my treatment my insurance company refused to pay for a bone marrow transplant. Ultimately, that denial was one of the greatest gifts God ever gave me, for it awakened in me a fighting spirit. I decided to go public with my fight. The support I received was unbelievable, both in support of my right to a transplant and the funding of it.

There is a beautiful song from the 1940's, called "Pennies From Heaven." That song reminds me of how it felt when money for my transplant suddenly began to materialize from many little corners of the world—it was truly heaven-sent.

✺

My sisters work in production at a General Motors plant. They hung this sign as they and their friends sold Sloppy Joes and baked goods: *We cooked all night, and we baked all day. We did it for Vickie, cuz her insurance won't pay.*

✺

A handwritten note with $10 from a single mom: "I wish it could be more. Every battle that you fight is one less my daughters will have to fight."

✺

AND MY CUP IS REFILLED

A phone call out of the blue: "My daughter and her family have been fighting this same insurance company issue silently and it's killing her—can she join you?"

✤

One day I received an envelope full of change—$2.78 to be exact. My 6-year-old niece, Mallory, had sent me her Disneyland money. I tried to send it back, but my brother said that she had bought what she wanted with that money.

✤

A young man at a school I visited: "Thank you, Vickie. My mom (who had cancer) had given up—now she says she'll fight some more."

✤

My nephew, Chad, called; he was doing a story on heroes and he wanted to use my story.

✤

In the checkout line at the grocery store: "You made me realize that this could happen to anyone."

✤

In another store: "I called my congressmen for the first time because you said that they must hear our voice if their vote is to reflect it."

🌿

My friend's daughter: "I'm proud that you weren't embarrassed to talk about it in public. At first I thought breast cancer was embarrassing; now I don't, it's just maddening."

🌿

In church: "You are on so many prayer lists—God just has to listen."

🌿

A college-age daughter of a friend: "Because of you, my friends and I started talking about breast cancer and our roles as women in the fight. We walked in the Relay for Health and were joined by some of the guys."

🌿

Being met at the airport with a "Welcome home, we love you!" banner, a rose, and hugs and kisses from Nicci and Chad after a treatment and test results.

🌿

A local Lioness Club called and asked me to come and share my views on breast cancer and what we as women need to do for ourselves. It was the first of what would eventually become hundreds of such talks. They gave me the courage to let my passion for the message override my fear of its delivery. In doing so they opened a new door in my life, and I will be forever grateful.

*

There are more, *far* more, good people in the world than bad. The bad just seem to be louder. Listen for the whispers.

*

Remember, those "pennies from heaven" come in many forms.

*

Through the years it has been an honor for me to share in the lives of so many cancer patients and their families. I've learned so many things from them. The gifts they have given to me—love, trust, support, encouragement, hope, and inspiration—are truly beyond measure. And there is one more cherished gift—they have given me their prayers.

One of the things we often say to each other is, "Keep me in your prayers." Over the years my own prayers have changed. Yes, I still pray for wellness and health for all, but always, always, always I pray for your peace. Peace of mind and heart are two of our greatest gifts, and I believe that the gateway to both leads through hope. I believe that God gave us the keys to His kingdom when He gave us the ability to hope. Our beloved chaplain at CTCA in Zion, Illinois, Rev. Percy McCray, loves to quote Hebrews 11:1 to us: "Faith is the substance of things *hoped* for, the evidence of things not seen."

Yes, even faith is rooted in hope, for hope must come first. So, I pray that within these pages you have found some things to bring you peace of mind and heart, and a tip or two for the body—but above all else I pray that you have found hope. May the message of hope shine through each and every word I've written. For I *have* walked the road ahead of you and I have come back to tell you that in the darkest of dark and in the deepest of despair there is hope—and where there is hope, *all things* are possible. Always remember, even when it is not probable, it is *possible* to win against this disease—of this I am living, breathing proof.

So, keep wearing the armor of hope, my friends. Keep fighting and keep supporting each other along the way. Keep your pilot lights on high and, in so doing, may God bless us, one and all.

Organizations, Events and Programs

American Cancer Society

1-800-ACS-2345   www.cancer.org

Contact the toll-free number or the website and you'll discover endless cancer treatment information, resources, publications, events and services, available both nationally and in your local area. *(If you are hoping that there is a certain program or advocate working on something you need, just call and there probably is!—Vickie)*

Cancer Treatment Centers of America (CTCA)

1-800-FOR-HELP   www.cancercenter.com

Mission Statement: We respond to patients and their families by offering world class treatment options that truly make a difference, delivered by the ablest and most compassionate professionals in a seamless and sensitive manner that empowers patients to make appropriate decisions and take management control of their disease. *(Well, folks, that pretty much says it all, and every word is true.—Vickie)*

Cancer Treatment Research Foundation (CTRF)

1-800-221-2873   www.ctrf.org

Mission Statement: Provide patients, survivors, and their families dignity, healing, and genuine hope for cure by sponsoring the world's most innovative and promising clinical research on science based treatment options. *(I look to this organization as my safety net. Ninety-seven cents of every dollar raised goes directly to research.—Vickie)*

Cancer Fighter Program
1-800-261-1255
A national program dedicated to making a difference in the fight against cancer for all people and for patients everywhere. It is an evening filled with information on cancer survival and prevention. Just gather 200 or more friends, neighbors, church members, etc. and we may send a speaker right to your community. *(Dr. Quillin, Rev. Percy McCray and yours truly are typical speakers in this program.—Vickie)*

Cancer Support Group Information
1-800-227-2345
(Attending a support group is a gift to yourself. Find a good one in your area by calling the American Cancer Society's toll free number above.—Vickie)

Reach to Recovery
1-800-227-2345
Sponsored by the American Cancer Society. Trained survivors visit women who have recently had a mastectomy, providing support, information and a bra. *(Staffed by incredibly caring people.—Vickie)*

Relay For Life
1-800-227-2345
A fantastic nationwide event sponsored by the American Cancer Society. *(This 24 hours will give you lasting support, encouragement and camaraderie. I strongly urge you to attend!— Vickie)*

Making Strides Against Breast Cancer
1-800-227-2345
If you are fighting breast cancer or are a survivor of breast cancer, this is a "must do" event for you. *(For all of you who love and support cancer survivors, this is a "should do" event for you too!—Vickie)*

Road To Recovery
1-800-227-2345
A wonderful "good Samaritan" program dedicated to helping cancer patients with transportation to doctor's offices and drug stores. Sponsored by the American Cancer Society.

Tell A Friend
1-800-227-2345
Participants in this program call five friends and ask them if they have had their mammogram. Encourage them to do so and follow up—it saves lives. Sponsored by the American Cancer Society. *(Go together and then have lunch!—Vickie)*

Walter Payton Cancer Fund
1-800-221-2873   www.payton34.org
The Payton family established the fund to honor Walter's life and to sponsor groundbreaking cancer research and creative treatment options. *(I believe these dedicated people are going to accomplish great things for all of us in the years to come.—Vickie)*

Girl Scouts of America
1-877-806-4870
Provides instruction and information to future generations to enable them to be responsible and caring adults, including critical education programs on breast cancer and prevention.

Lions International
1-630-571-5466
(This national community service organization provided me with my first speaking forums and has supported efforts to enlighten people everywhere to our own responsibilities to wellness.—Vickie)

Soroptomist International
1-215-557-9300   www.soroptomist.org
A worldwide organization for women in management and professions working through service projects to advance human rights and the status of women. *(Soroptomist is launching an important new women's health endeavor which will include the issues of breast and ovarian cancer.—Vickie)*

RECOMMENDED READING

Beating Cancer With Nutrition
by Patrick Quillin Ph.d, R.D., C.N.S.
1-800-247-6533   www.4nutrition.com
Clinically proven and easy-to-follow strategies to dramatically improve your quality and quantity of life and chances for a complete remission. *(This is my nutritional bible; do yourself a favor and add this weapon to your fight.—Vickie)*

Link to Life Newsletter
PO Box 964, Flint, MI 48501   www.link2life.com
A wonderfully informative and uplifting newsletter published by a very gifted ovarian cancer survivor. *(I write a column entitled, "Vickie's Spin" in each issue.—Vickie)*

NON-CANCER BOOKS
THAT I FOUND GREAT FOR CANCER PATIENTS

You've Got a Friend
by Dan Zadra
1-800-914-3327   www.compendiuminc.com
Thoughts to celebrate the joy of friendship. *(A treasured gift for any friend, whether battling cancer or not.—Vickie)*

Little Miracles
by Dan Zadra
1-800-914-3327   www.compendiuminc.com
Cherished messages of hope, joy, love, kindness and courage. *(Incredible book to lift your spirits and strengthen your resolve.—Vickie)*

God Calling
by A.J. Russell
A wonderful daily inspirational. *(It is so much more than that. It is written in today's language, and every page applies to everyday life. I strongly urge you to get a copy.—Vickie)*

Forever Remembered
by Dan Zadra
1-800-914-3327   www.compendiuminc.com
A Gift for the Grieving Heart. *(Cherished messages of hope, love and comfort from courageous people who have lost a loved one. This book touched me as few have. I will never be without a copy.—Vickie)*

ACKNOWLEDGMENTS

To my husband Rick who always believed I could get well, even when I didn't, thank you for helping me understand that all the healing powers do not come from the outside, but that many are found within ourselves. Thank you for talking until I listened. You too were a victim and are a survivor of this disease. For breast cancer attacked you as it has few others, trying to claim both your mother and your wife at the same time. I know the courage it took to lose one loved one, and then to have continued—without skipping a beat—to fight for the other. Few will ever understand what that cost you. Even I cannot fully imagine the pain. You stayed when you must have wanted to run, and you loved me knowing full well the price. We didn't always do it well, but we fought the fight together. For this and a million small things, I can never thank you enough. I hope it will somehow suffice to say that I love you.

To my parents who gave me so much more than love, please know that your priceless gifts of self-confidence, self worth, and pure determination were essential in my survival. You instilled tools in me throughout my childhood that I would later call upon to save my life. Whether you realize it or not you were with me every hour and every day of my fight in both my mind and my heart. And I knew then, as I do now, that you are never more than a phone call away. Thank you for being my eternal safety net. I love you both more than you can ever know.

To my family, some by blood and some by marriage, who stood with me and, at times, for me—thank you from the bottom of my heart. You made the fight worth fighting, but more than that, you made the hours and days during the fight worth living. You encouraged me to fight at each obstacle and, when possible, you physically removed those that stood in my way. You fought when you could, and you paid when I could not. You helped rally an army on my behalf. You came without my asking. If you could hear my cry then, I pray that you can now feel my gratitude and love, for they are beyond words. Especially, Pam and Geri, you were always there to help me rediscover the beauty of life and to help me distinguish it from the ugliness of this disease. Thank you, thank you, thank you; I love you all so much.

Special thanks to Mom and Dad, Pam, Gail, Curt, Jeff, Melinda, and Aunt Betty. You came, at great expense to your lives (not to mention your pocketbooks), and you stayed. When the hardest battle—the bone marrow transplant—began, you were my cavalry. You circled the wagons around Rick and me with love and support when we needed it most. I swear, the day you all arrived I heard the trumpets blow. Michelle, April, and Autumn, you may have had the hardest job of all, for you had to stay home when you wanted to come, because you were caring for three of my greatest reasons for fighting, while awaiting the arrival of another. But you were with me nonetheless. I felt your strength and prayers all the way from California and Michigan. And Dawn, the charge sounded once again when you came and brought me a fresh reserve of love and hope. Thank you all for being with me at my worst and for loving me through it. For 31 days I couldn't get out–so, with prayers and in gowns, masks, and gloves, when necessary, you came in.

I must give special thanks, also, to **Dr. Brian Bolwell**. As always, when I did not fit "protocol," you somehow revamped, overhauled, and made my transplant a perfect fit. You took me and my determination under your wing, despite insurance denials and lack of funds. How do I thank you, except to say that you are one of the "great ones" in expertise and in heart.

To my friends, some from childhood, some new, some still here and some gone, your love and kindness has colored every word I've written and every feeling I've had. Your love and support when I needed it most showed me that I am rich beyond measure. You gave me a priceless gift with your caring and you will never fully understand the strength I drew from that. If I live to be a hundred I will never forget how I felt at the benefit dance you held for me the night before my bone marrow transplant. Your love was stronger than any medicine, and I drew on it so many times to help me survive. The memory of all of us together is now, and will forever be, one of the best things in my entire life. All of you helped guide my steps from the darkness back out into the light. Thank you, and please know that I love you.

To Cancer Treatment Centers of America, please accept my deepest gratitude. You are my extended family in every sense of the word. You all fought for my life when no one else would. Without you, there would be no book because, without you, there would be no me. Thank you for seeing me as a living person and not a dying patient. I wish I had space to name everyone who made an incredible difference in saving my life. I'm afraid that would be a book in itself, but there are those I must mention:

First, the founder and chairman of Cancer Treatment Centers of America, **Richard Stephenson,** for without your dream of a better, more humane, comprehensive, and empowering way of treating cancer patients there would be no CTCA. You took your hopes and dreams for cancer patients everywhere and turned them into the reality that is CTCA. Thank you for knowing exactly what we, your patients, would need before we ourselves could identify it. And then for having it all in place waiting for us at our hour of greatest need. You have collected the best and brightest in the fields of cancer, nutritional and naturopathic treatments and have armed them with the latest in medical technology and research, on our behalf.

But thank you even more for understanding that it takes more than medical expertise, equipment, and research to win this battle. You knew that our minds, our hearts, and our souls must be supported, nurtured, and healed and you put an army of wonderfully gifted people in place to help us. Your dream has become a godsend to so many, a refuge in the worst of storms. Thanks for leveling the playing field and giving us our chance. I loved your heart before I ever met you and I now count it as one of life's blessings that I have the privilege of calling you friend.

Also a very special thank you and a heart full of love to one of the main keepers of the dream, **Dr. Alfonso Mellijor.** You were my first contact with CTCA; it could have all begun or ended with you.

Without your gentleness and encouragement I would've never met the rest of the team. I came to you, Doctor M, having been assured by so many that nothing awaited me but death, and in one meeting you gave me the beautiful gift of possibility. You turned me back from the abyss and gave me hope; you encouraged me to take a chance on life again. You fought for me, but above all else, you fought with me. At some point you became more than just my doctor, you became my friend and my life became richer for it. You walked, step by step, with me through the darkness of treatment out into the light of recovery. How does one thank someone for that? I'm not sure, but I try nightly.

And **Mara,** what can I possibly say to you? You were my nurse who became my friend. You have encouraged, scolded, supported, and nagged me from the first time that we bumped heads right up to today—please never stop. We have laughed, cried, shared unspoken fears, and jumped for joy together. We are now the closest of friends. Miles may distance our bodies, but never our hearts.

I could name so many more at CTCA: **Dr. Sanchez,** always, always there when I need you; **MaryLou, Mary, Elizabeth, Percy, and Amber.** The list goes on and on. Thank you for taking me into your care and your hearts. I have seen the slight fear in your eyes any time I have mentioned an ache or pain or faced re-eval. I know what it could cost you for having let me cross the line from patient to friend. I am more than just grateful for the added risk you are willing to take. Merely saying that I love all of you at Cancer Treatment Centers seems so inadequate, but love you I do.

Last, but not least, thank you **Dan Zadra,** my editor at Compendium publishing company, for helping me see my journey through your eyes and convincing me that this book could help others. Your encouragement, insight, and incredible ability to see to the heart of the matter made this book not just possible, but a pleasure to write. I am forever in your debt, my friend, for having turned up the flame on my pilot light.

To order additional copies of
There's No Place Like Hope, or to receive
a free catalog of Compendium products,
call or write today:

COM·PEN´·DI·UM™
Incorporated

Publishing and Communications

This book may be ordered directly from the
publisher, but please try your local bookstore first!
Call toll free (800) 91-IDEAS
6325 212th St. SW, Suite K
Lynnwood, WA 98036

www.compendiuminc.com